Getting Out of Line

Getting Out of Line

*A Guide for
Teachers Redefining
Themselves and
Their Profession*

Caren Black

CORWIN PRESS, INC.
A Sage Publications Company
Thousand Oaks, California

ACKNOWLEDGMENTS: *Material excerpted from* Inspiration Sandwich, *copyright © 1992 by SARK. Reprinted by permission of Celestial Arts, P.O. Box 7123, Berkeley, CA 94707. Material from the book* Way of the Peaceful Warrior *© 1984 by Dan Millman. Reprinted by permission of H J Kramer, P.O. Box 1082, Tiburon, CA 94920. All rights reserved. Material from* The Seat of the Soul *reprinted with the permission of Simon & Schuster from* The Seat of the Soul *by Gary Zukav. Copyright © 1989 by Gary Zukav.*

For information:

Corwin Press, Inc.
A Sage Publications Company
2455 Teller Road
Thousand Oaks, California 91320
E-mail: order@corwin.sagepub.com

SAGE Publications Ltd.
6 Bonhill Street
London EC2A 4PU
United Kingdom

SAGE Publications India Pvt. Ltd.
M-32 Market
Greater Kailash I
New Delhi 110 048 India

Printed in the United States of America

Library of Congress Cataloging-in-Publication Data

Black, Caren.
    Getting out of line : a guide for teachers redefining themselves and their profession / Caren Black.
        p. cm.
    Includes bibliographical references and index.
    ISBN 0-8039-6502-8 (cloth acid-free paper). — ISBN 0-8039-6503-6 (pbk. acid-free paper)
        1. Teaching—United States. 2. Teachers—United States. I. Title.
LB1775.2.B53 1997
    371.102—dc21   97-4859

This book is printed on acid-free paper.

97 98 99 00 01 02 03 10 9 8 7 6 5 4 3 2 1

Corwin Press Production Editor: S. Marlene Head
Editorial Assistant: Kristen L. Gibson
Typesetters: Laura A. and William C. E. Lawrie
Cover Designer: Marcia R. Finlayson

Contents

Foreword

In this unique and provocative examination of teachers and the teaching profession, Caren Black calls upon teachers to redefine themselves—to determine what it means to be a teacher. Drawing from an eclectic mix of research in education, business, the new physics, futurist theory, and her own 20 years on the educational front lines, Black finds striking parallels as she guides the reader toward a new definition of teaching. Black intends to stimulate professional dialogue and encourage self-reflection. She will surely succeed on both counts. Not a book to curl up with in bed (it's far too stimulating to induce sleep!), *Getting Out of Line* is a book for all who care deeply about children and education. Replete with inspirational stories, thought-provoking parables, and memorable quotes, it's a book to read, ponder, and debate in faculty meetings, teacher support groups, and educational seminars. In this era of school reform in which, too often, outside reformers step inside a school and work with teachers to alter the school culture, Black offers a refreshing alternative. Change, she believes, must occur from within the school and, first and foremost, within the psyche of every individual teacher.

Is our current school-as-factory model of education obsolete? In her opening chapter, Black argues convincingly that it is and that we've known this to be true for more than a decade. Rather than adjust to a new reality (Black admits that change, even positive change, can be painful), educators have simply tinkered with the old system through myriad reform initiatives, "innovative" programs, and changes mandated by bureaucrats who may never step inside a classroom. Black minces no words about one point: Teachers are the ones who must redefine themselves and their profession. So how can teachers effect real change? What does it take to redefine teaching in a way that meshes with the new understandings regarding human learning and development?

Black maintains that the redefinition of teaching begins with teachers' developing an attitude about themselves as educators. Delightfully opinionated, Black urges her readers to develop their own strong opinions. She wants teachers to think, to challenge the status quo, to define and determine their own professional destinies. In so doing, Black explains, teachers will claim the voice, the self-confidence, and the self-respect that are the hallmarks of true professionals. Indeed, it's the imposed inability to make decisions, form opinions, or claim a voice that has led to teacher passivity, powerlessness, and a lack of professionalism.

Once teachers alter their personal attitudes about who they are as teachers, they must necessarily reconsider how they teach. To help her readers meet this challenge, Black lists the conditions for optimal learning under three primary categories. Learning occurs best when it's (1) personal, (2) natural, and (3) cyclical.

As a talented classroom teacher, Black has little patience for those who waste her precious teaching time and her students' learning time. Accordingly, she doesn't waste her readers' time. Readers move quickly from a discussion of theory to the Monday-morning reality of the classroom. What to do? How to survive? Black offers cogent advice and stirring examples as she describes effective instructional strategies that support and enable a new definition of teaching.

She devotes the last chapter to learning models. Drawing on her experiences and expertise as an arts educator and the director of a children's theater, she outlines the intriguing ACTS (Applied Curriculum Teaching Strategies) model. The premise is simple. The best education is real—the *stuff* of life, not just preparation for life. Students have opportunities to work collaboratively, make choices, and present their understandings to others.

In conclusion, Black warns that change is never easy, but as teachers become redefined *New* Teachers, they can look forward to increased self-respect as well as more personal power and freedom and a greater sense of accomplishment. Silenced no more, in touch with their own prowess, they can reach out to help students discover their own inner capabilities. For it is only after teachers believe in the potential of every teacher, including themselves, that they can hope to find the potential in every student. And that is, after all, what teaching is all about.

LOIS BRIDGES
The Galef Institute

Preface:
Creating a Personal Vision of Change

Two days ago, a good friend of mine, an extremely intelligent and capable young woman, told me she wants to leave teaching. Inwardly, I felt despair that the very kind of person whom we need in public education should feel fed up and want to leave. Outwardly, I simply asked her to tell me why. Immediately she replied that it isn't the kids or the teaching but the lack of respect and control she feels, the often untenable conditions that continue year after year. She summed it up in one word: "stress"—or, as she so eloquently put it, "the stress of not being able to change an intolerable situation."

Change, being life's only constant, is a tool of learning, evidence of growth, Nature's signature of Life. The ability to author change is an expression of personal freedom and autonomy, whereas "continuous inability to make a difference leads to withdrawal" (Fullan, 1993, p. 55).

Peter Senge wrote in 1990: "People don't resist change. They resist being changed" (p. 155). My friend, like many other teachers, would like to effect changes she sees as necessary for the good of her students, but she cannot because her judgment is rendered irrelevant by the system she works under. Meanwhile, both she and her situation—her room, her students, her work requirements—are being changed as mandated by people who've never worked in or visited her classroom, often by people who have never taught at all. When these changes are unworkable or counterproductive for her students, her only real options are to implement them anyway (or pretend to)—or leave.

My own optimism, with which I began this work over a year ago, has also faltered a bit as I have watched the system operate against the enthusiastic and valiant efforts of so many teachers like my friend. But my loss of optimism is probably a good thing, because what remains is *hope*. Tom Athanasiou (1996) uses the terms in relation to the challenges facing our world: *optimism* "tilts almost inevitably toward complacency, naivete" (p. 104), whereas *hope* implies a basis in realism with some plan of action.

As educators, we are all caught in the maelstrom of changes and reforms sweeping our profession. But these changes and reforms do not equal *real change*. For what we see in public education is not the change of the paradigm shift (a term that's been beaten and misused until rendered senseless) or any other kind of fundamental change. Instead, it is a series of desperate attempts for greater control by and of the wrong people. Increasing the changes being mandated upon a group of people (teachers) while decreasing their status creates a powerful symbiosis, a self-perpetuating spiral that transmogrifies rather than transforms.

The reformers—politicians, bureaucrats, administrators, school board members, professors, consultants, parents, and even teachers—assume that if we are diligent enough in our use of resources (more new technology, research, laws), both to closely monitor student progress (more new assessment "yardsticks") *and* to give teachers more training (more new programs, more materials, more techniques), we will ultimately produce the desired level of student achievement. It seems like sound logic, but it's actually as effective as trying to drive a car from the back seat and as revealing (in terms of comprehending *change*) as Ramona's rendition of the "dawnzer lee light" song (Cleary, 1968).

If anything more substantial than a gnawing acquaintance with our inner child has come from the self-help movement, it is that the only true change we can make is to change ourselves—our own inner selves. Backseat drivers try to construct and control change *through other people,* to "teacher-proof" classroom instruction. Simultaneously and oxymoronically, they define current desirable teachers characteristics through their literature and job descriptions: a lifelong learner, a critical thinker, student-centered, good communication skills, a team player, solid literacy teaching skills, certification to teach English as a second language, computer literate, and willing to try new ideas and take risks. The dilemma is that someone with these qualifications is not going to enjoy being teacher-proofed!

Today's *actual* definition of teacher is closer to this: "someone who annually implements, integrates, individualizes, diversifies, enhances, translates, compacts, animates, and writes curriculum, while maneuvering endless hoops and hurdles, maintaining a positive attitude and enormous energy, and thriving on the challenge of the seemingly impossible. See *Don Quixote*."

We need a redefinition of who a teacher is, one that supports change, not tinkering, one that reflects the all-encompassing global change of the era in which we live. We need to define what such a *New* Teacher is expected—*and empowered*—to do.

Such a definition must come from teachers themselves if it is to have any lasting value. This book offers a guide toward that definition, not "the" new method nor step-by-step directions on "how to," but self-help and support for teachers willing to reframe that magical interaction between someone who has knowledge she wants to share and someone who wants to learn.

This book is about dignity and personal responsibility. In it, I attempt to examine things no one tells you before you become a teacher and no one talks about afterward. I present a model from my work in the performing arts and my recent research, which may serve teachers as a filter for evaluating programs and practice. I also discuss the *change* we must unavoidably make for ourselves, our students, our world.

Acknowledgments

The ideas presented represent extensive research into the literature of education, business, the new physics, and futurist theory, as well as considerable input from teachers, teacher educators, administrators, and students in schools I have observed, taught in, or managed during the past 20 years. To these people, and many others, I owe great thanks. Gunnar Benson, Dr. Lois Bridges, Sharon Dale, Dr. Guy Duckworth, Gus Giordano, Dr. Leslie Hinderyckx, Dr. Barbara McIntyre, Earl Ricker, Dr. Stephanie Steffey, and Dr. William Zachmeier are visionary, inspirational educators. I'd especially like to thank Dr. Marty Krovetz of San Jose State University for his guidance in the research and publication of this work. Thank to Alice Foster and Marlene Head at Corwin Press, Dr. Marsha Speck, John Bernardi and Jeanette Ferris, and my husband, Russ Stemple, all of whom played a vital role in bringing this book to print. Finally, to all teachers reading this book: *Thank you for all you give every day.* May you get something back here.

We can do nothing to stop the forces of change currently transforming our lives and the world. It is folly to try to hide from or deny them, to turn back the digital clock to a time more fondly remembered, to attempt escape. But we can embrace the changes, and in doing so, *direct* them, be the solution, not the problem. We can define our challenging and often overwhelming point in history as an exhilarating time to be alive!

CAREN BLACK
Aptos, CA

About the Author

Caren Black has taught for more than 20 years in various fields, including piano, dance, creative dramatics, musical theater, small business start-up, middle school math and humanities, second grade, and K–3 team-taught, nongraded classes. Currently, she teaches a Grade 3–4 class. She holds a bachelor's in piano and a master's in theater from Northwestern University, a master's in educational administration from San Jose State University, and California teaching and administrative credentials as well as a Cross-Cultural, Language, and Academic Development certificate.

In 1995, Black completed a qualitative research study, *Pedagogy of the New Teacher*. In 1972, she researched *A Study of the Elements Common to Dance, Drama and Music as a Framework for a Combined Arts Curriculum*. She also has written and produced two children's musicals. Interrupting her teaching career in the 1980s, Black worked for a decade in business, beginning at MGM/UA in Los Angeles and ending as a small business teacher and consultant for the Central Coast Small Business Development Center. She lives in Aptos, California, with her husband Russ and two cats, Kona and Mikey (who commutes to school with her to work in her classroom).

In memory of Carson DeJarnett,
who never gave up until we understood.

1

Preparing to Live in a Different Reality

So quickly that few have recognized what is happening, a society that lasted for ten thousand years has begun to dissolve. In its place a new society has been growing up, one in which the mores, habits, and goals of a hundred centuries are being profoundly altered. Some might take longer than others to recognize this colossal reorientation; many will undoubtedly spend the rest of their lives resisting the new direction of humanity. But it is real.

WILLIAM GLASSER (IN LAND & JARMAN, 1992, P. 72)

Few would argue that great change is occurring within our lives and our world. In a single lifetime, world population has quadrupled, 70% of all bird species are in decline, as much as half of the topsoil of some of the earth's best farming areas (like Iowa) is now at the bottom of the ocean. On the positive side, many people have gained democracy, new freedoms, and greater civil rights, and the individual has more power to pursue learning and to exchange ideas, goods, and services with more people in more places than ever before. Although each of these changes in itself is profound, cumulatively they only begin to scratch the surface of what is now going on. Before we can redefine our life's work in teaching, we must understand the depth—and force—of change taking place in our world.

Defining Reality

This depth and force of change involve far more than a list of changes, the rate of change, or the number of people involved. Though these are all quite impressive, they are not the root, merely little green shoots catching our attention. The root is nothing less than our current level of thinking, our culture's way of viewing the world—what we think of as "real" or "true." Change like this occurs because it has to, and the universe has a way of doing what is necessary. We are preparing to live in a different reality. The terms seem oxymoronic, but are not. Very different cultures perceive the world very differently. The same culture changes its perception when "times" change drastically. A culture's perception, its view of the way the world works and people's place in the world, defines what happens within that culture, in exchanges with other cultures, and more recently, to the earth itself. Five hundred years ago, Western culture viewed reality quite differently from the way we see it now (see Table 1.1).

The Age of Reason: A Culture Defines Our Recent Past

The Age of Reason, the Renaissance, the Age of Enlightenment, the Age of Exploration—the names overlay each other in describing a period of less than 350 years when tremendous change and expansion lifted Europe out of a feudal agrarian culture and thrust it into the Industrial Revolution. For our purposes, I will use the *Age of Reason* to encompass the process that caused an entire society to redefine the world around—and within—it. What was real; what was not. What worked; what didn't. What was right, and wrong.

As an agrarian culture, Europeans had been tied to the land and saw themselves as part of nature, planting and harvesting by the cycles of the moon, and reading the stars, the land, the oceans, the winds, and their fellow creatures. Time was cyclical; the "hour" referred to a position of the sun. Time's passage was marked by events in the vast space of the heavens. There was much in life that remained a mystery and was assumed best left as such.

Although predominantly Christian, society held onto remnants of so-called pagan beliefs, for example, that all living creatures have spirits and some type of consciousness. Magic, wizardry, and sorcery were far from being just children's fantasies. People were born

TABLE 1.1 Western Cultural Views of Reality in Different Eras

	Medieval Times	Age of Reason	Information Age
Time	Cyclical	Linear	Relative
Nature	Includes humans	Under human domain	Includes humans
Reason	From instinct, feelings	Superior to instinct, feelings	Works with instinct, feelings
Knowledge	From experience, faith; limited	From dissection, segmentation; unlimited	From whole, systemic study; unlimited
Worker	Life station	To be controlled, directed	To think, make decisions
Learning	Acquired through experience, practice	Received in incremental, logical sequences and by examination	Personally, experientially constructed

to a station in life; it was best to aspire to no other. It was ludicrous to think of any single human individual as being of particular importance, except loved ones and the reigning monarch.

It was into this milieu that the "New Age thinkers" of *those* times thrust their linear, rational, logical thoughts. Newton's new laws of physical science made the universe mechanical, like a giant clock, not magical any longer. Everything (it was assumed) could (sooner or later) be broken down into its basic building blocks and thus understood, manipulated, and ultimately controlled. Best practice for nearly any kind of work became a step-by-step, incremental approach using "detached" observation, "objective" experimentation, and final "impartial" analysis of results.

People began to think of time as linear more than cyclical, measured by clocks more than the heavens, with hours identified numerically, rather than by positions of the sun.

Space too became a separate three-dimensional phenomenon, the measurement of which took on new significance. Matter, it was determined, had mass, was solid, and was acted upon by another separate phenomenon called force or energy. The interactions of the two could be observed and charted in separate, linear fashion as cause and effect. No more powers or creatures that could not be rationally and consistently observed through the use of the five senses.

No more ancient mysteries to be explained through legend or accepted on faith. Life's unanswerable questions were reduced to mere problems to be solved in due time through methodical research and experimentation.

The philosophies of Descartes and others exalted the (civilized, human) individual for (his) ability to reason and to tame "brutish" emotion, which clouded logic. The Humanists separated people from the natural world. Da Vinci designed flying machines and painted the hand of God touching the hand of man. Michelangelo carved statues glorifying the human form. Humankind—or at least *man*kind—had a newfound, unlimited, individual potential and importance, and the earth, its resources, and its creatures were at humanity's disposal, waiting to be controlled and consumed.

Adam Smith's concept of national wealth and his laws governing its accumulation held that goods and services traded measured a nation's worth. This undoubtedly cheered those New Agers on voyages of exploration or in the new trading (shipping) companies.

However, it changed holy hillsides, haunted woods, and magic lakes into prime real estate valued in gold, not legends. Although these earthshaking ideas seem commonplace to us because we have grown up in a culture based on them, they drastically changed the entire world by creating a new Western culture and beginning an Age of Exploration, which touched indigenous cultures on every inhabited continent, often either acculturating or destroying them.

It's hard for us to grasp how new these ideas were and how significantly they changed the world, because to us they are simply "the way things are" or "the truth." *This is what a cultural paradigm is.* Despite its common and erroneous use as a buzzword for "new idea," a *paradigm* is "a constellation of concepts, values, perceptions, and practices shared by a community, which forms a particular vision of reality that is the basis of the way the community organizes itself" (Capra, 1996, p. 6). Our cultural *paradigm* is nothing short of what our entire society accepts as "reality" or "fact," the *way* we view life. It permeates everything we do, see, and believe in, and is as difficult for us to observe with detachment as water for a fish. Nevertheless, it is not the only view of reality, and there is much evidence that it is no longer the best or even the right view.

How can this be? How can there be more than one reality when Newtonian science has taught us that reality is "out there" and constant? Einstein taught that ideas about the physical world are determined in the human mind and not, as it would seem, by the external world. This can be very threatening stuff. However, it should help to realize that we are not the first to face a cultural paradigm shift, that the reality we take for granted—and now must let go of—was once very threatening for our ancestors to embrace, that such radical cultural change is a natural process, and that—provided we do not fight it—we will survive and come out on the other side. Finally, as we begin to understand the *cultural* change we face, we may perceive the educational changes we need to make as both less threatening and of different kinds than we previously thought.

The Age of Information: We Redefine Reality

The comfortable and familiar ideas of the Age of Reason would seem to have served us well. In a moment, we will look at how they were applied to create a system of public education that has been incredibly successful in training staggering numbers of people to function in, and contribute to, the world as we have envisioned it. Many say that we have the most advanced and educated culture in the history of the world. Others have begun to question the definition of *advanced*. They would say that when our 5% of the world's population consumes 30% of the world's resources and produces twice its own collective body weight in waste daily (Gore, 1993, p. 147), the worldview that produced this situation is no longer sustainable, that to change our way of life is not only inevitable, but essential.

This new change with which we are now struggling began with theories and discoveries made during the first half of the 20th century. Whether or not we realize it, the second half of that century has touched us all in coming to terms with the change these ideas imply. The central force behind these ideas was Albert Einstein. Thanks to Einstein's relativity theory and the work of the many quantum physicists who built on it, Newton's radical changes in natural laws have been changed again, just as profoundly.

Time is no longer linear but relative, and not separate from but bound inseparably to space in a *four*-dimensional continuum. Seemingly solid matter is not so solid anymore; vast amounts of space actually fill the molecules of which it is composed. Like time and space, mass and energy are seen to be not separate phenomena but different forms of the same one. The interconnectedness, interdependence, and intereffectiveness of all phenomena are being accepted. The basic building blocks of the universe have turned out to be not the separate, irreducible units of matter Newton postulated, but "probability patterns" (Capra, 1983, p. 91), at times particles, at times waves, depending, in part, on the experimenter's expectations and presence, which cannot be entirely separated from the results of observation or experimentation. (So much for detached objectivity.) In addition, the hologram, with each of its tiniest pieces reflecting the whole, has replaced Newton's mechanical clock as the metaphor for the universe.

As though to underscore the cyclical nature of our new thinking and negate the linear view we are growing out of, we are once again ready to accept the reality of phenomena and forces that we cannot measure with five senses. We are willing to permit the possibility that there are more than five senses and more than one "intelligence." Likewise, we see the need for more than one measurement of IQ.

We now realize that as humans we are not separate from nature, nor do we have the right to dispose of, or the means to control, the earth, its resources and creatures. Scientists like Fritjof Capra show humans, and all of nature, as part of extremely complex, interdependent biological or eco- systems. Our new quest is becoming not control, but responsibility—for ourselves and for how our actions affect the earth and other beings both now and in the future. Change, which was "a step-by-step incremental process," is now seen as constant, cyclical, "the creative process [forming] the dynamic of all nature" (Land & Jarman, 1992, pp. 98-99).

Medical researchers and professors like Antonio R. Damasio (1994) are finding evidence in the brain that, contrary to the Cartesian theory of reason's superiority over emotion, these two human capacities must work together for us to function as whole human beings. Even Adam Smith's entrenched concept of material wealth is at last being questioned, both as to its sustainability and its credibility.

Aided by the new physics, the ancient idea that all living beings have a soul, a spirit, and/or consciousness is regaining ground. This belief, of course, was not limited to the Druids in Medieval England but is universal in nearly every culture in the world. In fact, so many parallels have arisen between the new physics and ancient beliefs, for example, Taoism, that there has been a resurgence of interest in ancient Eastern and indigenous philosophies.

And we haven't even discussed technology yet! The globalization of communications means that two "ordinary" individuals (in terms of technologically developed or developing countries), regardless of race, sex, age, or impairment, can exchange ideas or conduct business—from their homes, if they wish—on any day at any time in any language without supervision, interference, or direct regulation by anyone else. This is incredible individual power, choice, connectedness. Such micro exchanges, coupled with macro transactions—for example, the globalization of business—are already eroding the importance of concepts like national boundaries and currencies well beyond anything dreamed of or accounted for by Adam Smith.

What our future will be and, indeed, whether we will have one depends, many say, on our current ability to completely shift our thinking in line with these new ideas. To paraphrase a popular Einstein quote: The world that we have made as a result of the level of thinking we have done thus far creates problems that we cannot solve at that same level of thought.

Reality Defines the Workplace

In the Age of Reason, of course, the new reality and its new ways of thinking were not available to everyone, nor were they meant to be. They were the domain of European, Christian, white male gentry. Concurrent with the new beliefs was a somewhat contrasting one: that man was by nature both brutish and lazy, and prone to the baser instincts and behaviors, needing both civilization and salvation. The noblesse oblige were to first convert those less civilized (in European opinion) to Christianity and then to "uplift" them through religious and secular education as well as worldly industry (continual, hard work; Margolin, 1989).

This opinion of human nature greatly influenced the treatment of other species (who were considered uncivilized and so were by definition "lesser") and of native inhabitants of colonial lands (who were "without religion" and "without civilization" when theirs did not conform to European standards/worldview).

It also applied to workers. The business practices that grew out of the Age of Reason, and this view of workers, are of great significance to teachers. For, in the Industrial Revolution that followed the Age of Reason, workers were no better off than serfs had been in the Middle Ages. It was the responsibility of management (so management "reasoned") to keep these people "in line" (this became literal), to train them or at least to institute rules and procedures that deterred lapses into their expected, undesirable behaviors. The Newtonian idea of breaking things down into step-by-step, linear approaches to tasks, the idea of human separation from nature and control of resources and "lesser" humans—in short, the cultural paradigm of the Age of Reason was encapsulated in what became the symbol of Industrialism: the assembly line.

The Assembly Line: A Model Defines the Age

Before the Industrial Revolution, master shoemakers had crafted single pairs of shoes on demand for individual customers, sometimes from the customers' own leather. Style, fit, and purpose were all individualized and the relationship between *custom* and *customer*, obvious.

On the assembly line, hundreds of people made thousands of pairs of shoes, for people they would never meet, from raw material purchased by someone else from the lowest bidder. Packagers, advertisers, shippers, warehousers, wholesalers, store managers, and sales clerks brought the shoes to the retail customer. Style, fit, and purpose could no longer be customized, but that was compensated for by increased selection and lower cost.

The whole process took less time, employed more people, and cost the customer less than ever before. The economy expanded, jobs were created, and more people could afford a higher standard of living. No wonder the assembly line, as later perfected by Frederick Winslow Taylor and implemented by Henry Ford in America, became the model for so many other fields besides manufacturing.

Note its familiarity. The assembly line required that workers stay in line along a conveyor belt. Raw leather passed by worker after worker, each adding the particular graduated process for which she or he was trained until leather was turned into shoes. Anywhere along the line workers could drop out defective shoes; shoes that made it to the end of the line had to pass a final examination by inspectors.

Workers on the assembly line were paid (quite little) for quick and accurate repetition of the same task, *not for thinking*. Their position and purpose were underscored by their pay, which increased not by what they knew or could contribute, but by *how long they continued to do the same thing in the same place*. A flowchart of managers and bosses did the thinking and told the workers what to do and how to do it. The low level of thought and responsibility desired of workers on the line allowed even children to be employed in Dickensian fashion (until the law forbade it) and kept such jobs in low esteem.

Although the assembly-line factory model was an ingenious economic advance, there were also a good many things wrong with it. In the 1940s, W. Edwards Deming and Joseph M. Juran documented many problems, such as workers' ability to "control fewer than 15% of the problems" (Scholtes, 1988, p. 112). Thus, workers can see and must deal with, either firsthand or indirectly, the other 85%, but they have no voice in their solution. This situation contributes to low worker morale. Low morale affects output.

In his training, Deming told a story very similar to this:

It was a Thursday morning around 9 am when Joe heard a "clink" and saw a shiny object exit the cutting blade on top of the line of fabric on which he worked. Joe told his supervisor, who didn't see anything and told Joe to get back to work.

Before long, Joe was aware that about every 10th bolt of fabric he cut would get a snag in it, running the length of the fabric. He told his supervisor he thought the blade was broken. The supervisor told Joe to get back to work, then went to tell the foreman.

One week later, a vice-president read a report showing sales were down due to defects in the fabric. Then the v-p of shipping noted numerous returns. The two v-p's complained to the factory v-p, who said he'd take care of it. Meanwhile, Joe muttered to himself, "The blankety-blank blade's broken."

The factory v-p called Joe's foreman to his office and gave him strict orders to speed up the line to produce more good product. Joe noticed every 5th bolt had a snag and muttered to himself, "The blankety-blank blade's broken."

The foreman was upbraided and told to correct the situation, so he had everyone work overtime. Joe noticed about every 3rd bolt had the snag. The factory v-p met with the two lower v-p's and asked them why the problem wasn't fixed. They didn't know. The company president got wind of the problem and called them all in. They told him they were sure they'd have the situation under control shortly and there would be no need to close down the line.

Now, every other bolt was snagged. Joe told other line workers about the blade. They already knew, but didn't think the supervisor or foreman would listen to any of them at this point. They were working double shifts at double time and still half the product was flawed.

The president decided to take matters into his own hands. He called an outside consultant. The consultant asked to go down to the floor and watch the line in progress. He walked around and studied the weary faces, heard the faint mutterings. "What do you think the problem is?" he asked Joe. "The blankety-blank blade's broke—Sir," added Joe quietly.

The line was stopped, the blade replaced and the snag disappeared from the fabric.

The point Deming made with such stories, of course, was that no one knows how to fix problems like the people who experience them firsthand.

Hierarchical administrative chains of command are far too inefficient and time-consuming for today's world. Inconsistencies in raw material create inconsistencies in end products and increase rejects. Separation from end consumers can increase consumer dissatisfaction with products. Preoccupation with the current quarter's report ignores costly long-term effects. In *The End of Bureaucracy and the Rise of the Intelligent Organization* (1994), Gifford and Elizabeth Pinchot delineate why bureaucracy is no longer an appropriate or workable system.

However, in the 1940s no one in American manufacturing listened to either Deming or Juran. Instead, both men went to help a defeated, occupied nation put its war-destroyed manufacturing base back together, and by the 1980s Japan was the world's leading manufacturing power, boldly utilizing Information-Age thinking in glaring contrast with the U.S. Industrial-Age system still in place. It was then that American manufacturing businesses began to listen. Eagerly.

The Worker: Redefinition Adds Value

Thanks to people like Deming and Juran (and severe economic threats), American business has taken its first baby steps toward a new worldview. Quality programs emphasize many of the ideas of the new cultural paradigm. One of the primary threads running through Deming's famous Fourteen Points is new respect for and power to workers. Workers think, give opinions, are listened to and have real decision-making power because *no one else has their direct access to information.* Today, Joe could simply stop the line when he heard the clink and have the blade checked and replaced. He wouldn't have to get permission or wait in silence, hoping to be listened to "someday." Worker ideas and contributions add value to a product rather than get in the way of the process. Workers are given real incentives (like a true voice and even a piece of the company) rather than false ones (like slogans, numerical score targets, and teas).

Workers can communicate with each other and work on teams that have true control of individual projects (including budget) from start to finish, rather than working always in isolation and under tight external regulation.

Relegating mind-numbing tasks to robots and exporting un-skilled tasks to less educated laborers (outsourcing) give workers the time and opportunity to grow, to advance, to use and expand their skills and knowledge, thereby becoming even more valuable to their company. Slashing middle management and flattening chains of command (downsizing) while employing new communications technologies links workers directly to each other, to management, to sources of information, and even to customers (or at least to cus-tomer information).

The new power and status of individual worker contributions is revealed in a recent *Wall Street Journal* report, "How Ford Cut Costs on Its 1997 Taurus, Little by Little" (Suris, 1996). Ford asked workers for cost-cutting suggestions and accepted worker-initiated cuts from as little as 10¢ to $7.85 per car, adding up to a potential savings for Ford of over $73 million annually.

Applying Redefinition to Schools

It's time to compare our all-encompassing, redefining change (cultural paradigm shift) with what is "passing" for change in the public schools and to decide what we, individually and together, can do about it. To begin, it's easy to see how the assembly line became the model for public schools, processing "raw material" through lin-ear grades with the expectation of uniform results at the end of the line.

However, today our raw material is less uniform than ever before; it's no longer practical to reject products along the line or at the end of the process, and a much more self-directed and individu-alized end product is expected. Clearly, our public education model is out of sync with our present and future reality. That's why changes and reforms, like the ones running rampant through edu-cation, are predestined for ultimate failure: they do not touch the model itself nor, to use Einstein's phrase, the level of thinking that created it. It isn't possible to ride a dead horse better, no matter what we try.

To create all aspects of a new model—one that fits the redefinition of reality—will require more than the efforts of teachers alone, but for many reasons, it must begin with teachers. First, no one else really knows what's going on in the classroom. Second, teachers have been silent about too many issues for too long, rendering vital information unavailable. (We will examine some of the issues and reasons for silence in Chapter 2.) Third, administration is not going to or cannot make the necessary changes. Unlike American manufacturing, public school administration has, as yet, no direct competition, no economic threat severe enough to force abdication of the current reality.

The point is that we must fully comprehend that change really means something far different from the current cacophony in public education, gain encouragement and power from the force of change surrounding us in our society, and find the means to redefine the core of education—our part of the new model: to redefine teaching.

2

Overcoming the Culture of Powerlessness

I have a serious suggestion to make. We should stop worrying about the problems of education, declare it a disaster, and let teachers and students get on with their lives. The trouble with the endless concern over "problems" in education is that many well-meaning but often misguided and sometimes meddlesome people believe that solutions must exist. They waste their own and other people's time and energy trying to find and implement these solutions. Typically, they try harder to do more of something that is already being done (although what is being done is probably one of the problems).

However, if education is a disaster, then it is not a collection of problems to be "solved," and trying to "improve" what we are already doing will only make the situation worse. You don't find solutions to disasters —you try to extricate yourself and other people from them. The way to survive a disaster is to do something different.

FRANK SMITH (1995, PP. 585-586)

Doing something different requires a change of attitude. Attitude is not merely a way of looking at something; it helps shape what's being viewed. As we learn from the new physics, attitude helps us to define the observed, its effect on us, and our effect on it. In Chapter 1 we saw how education arrived at the state Frank Smith describes as a disaster. The assembly-line model, on which our system is based, encapsulates the thought of a previous age and is no longer in sync with what we now know to be best practice or the way reality works. For well over a decade, we have, as Smith indicates, tinkered within this model and its resulting system. With the sole exception of the Commonwealth of Kentucky (which declared its school system unconstitutional and started over in 1990), public school reforms have not touched the system itself. None has examined the reality defining it.

Analyzing Our Position

The position of assembly-line worker is at the bottom of a long chain of command. (Even a school district with only one school has a board, a county board and superintendent, and myriad state and federal departments, boards, administrators, and legislators, all affecting the transaction that takes place between teachers and students.) Although production would have to stop without them, line workers are assumed to be interchangeable and replaceable parts. Individually, they do not have the autonomy, the bargaining power, or the status that professionals have. It's impossible from their position.

Professionals: Working in a New Culture

CPAs, doctors, lawyers, financial analysts, engineers, designers, programmers, consultants, and other professionals enjoy autonomy based more on the size of their employer and the strength of their own reputation than on the type of work they do. For example, an experienced, self-employed CPA will simply make and act on decisions (though she may consult with colleagues for a second opinion), whereas a junior CPA with a large firm will need to get approval first. Teachers, on the other hand, often go through the same approval process regardless of their experience or their school's size. Furthermore, a teacher new to a district but with 15 years' experience teaching in three countries, 10 years in international business, a master's in education, and an MBA can receive as much as $20,000 less per year than a teacher in the next room who has been in the same room, school, district, and grade level for 25 years and has a bachelor's degree.

Professionals subscribe to professional journals as opposed to magazines, market their abilities both within their firms and without, and freely choose among professional associations, seminars, and conferences that can keep them up-to-date, competitive, and growing. Their pay depends upon their negotiation skills, experience, competence, and the size of their firm. They can move "up the ladder" (because there is one) or go into business for themselves. If they change employers, they do not "lose" years of experience along with seniority, and it may be quite possible for them to arrive at a new job with an excellent reputation already in place.

Probably the biggest factor defining professionals is choice. One can choose to follow a career path by taking on more work; vying for the best projects; establishing a reputation; staying abreast of innovations; networking; striving toward advancement, a partnership, or one's own firm. Or one can choose a kind of respectable, stable anonymity in a large firm—or anything in between. Choice is available; it comes with the territory. Education and skills are, after all, supposed to increase choice.

Teachers: Working in a Time Warp

Because of their current "line worker" position within the model of the old paradigm, teachers have little in common with professionals. This is why efforts to "professionalize" teaching merely result in more duties, a process termed *intensification*: "pressures accumulate and innovations multiply under conditions of work that fail to keep pace with these changes and even fall behind. Under this view, the rhetoric of professionalism simply seduces teachers into consorting with their own exploitation" (Hargreaves, 1994, p. 15).

Like reform efforts that fail to address the systemic model, professionalization efforts fail because they add duties for, rather than changing the position of, teachers. Meanwhile, restructuring and reform efforts continue to produce programs with step-by-step approaches, with more and more training required—to teacher-proof materials. "The lack of intellectual ambition forced on schoolteachers . . . produces a smallness of personal presence" and "[The] stigmata of inferior status catch up to them quickly," observes 30-year veteran John Taylor Gatto (1995, pp. 4, 7), former New York State Teacher of the Year and author of *Dumbing Us Down* (1992). How do we, as teachers, break this pattern and redefine teaching to fit with the new worldview, while still working within a system built on the old one?

Changing Our Position

We begin with ourselves. Remember what the airlines tell us: In the event of a disaster, put your own oxygen mask on first, before attempting to place an oxygen mask on any children traveling with you. Teacher "instinct" is to help others first. We most often become teachers in the first place because we want to contribute, to make a difference. Fullan (1993) concurs and cautions:

> If concerns for making a difference remain at the one-to-one and classroom level, it cannot be done. . . . It must be seen that one cannot make a difference at the interpersonal level unless the problem and solution are enlarged to encompass the conditions that surround teaching . . . and the skills and actions that would be needed to make a difference. Without this additional and broader dimension the best of teachers will end up as moral martyrs. In brief, care must be linked to a broader social, public purpose . . . propelled by the skills of change agentry. (p. 11)

It's important to know how to contribute, to look at the big picture. Our instinct to give must be tempered first with self-preservation to be effective. To move out of position, to redefine teaching, we must become a new kind of teacher, one who assumes the voice and the respect, as well as the responsibilities, of a new paradigm professional. Gatto (1995) affirms that this is "the heart of the problem: We need to reinvent the teacher. We need teachers we never had" (p. 3). To do so requires a new attitude, one of greater self-confidence, self-respect, higher morale. To get there, let us reexamine just who and where we actually are in the greater scheme of things.

Self-Image: Changing Ours

In the opening statement by Frank Smith, we find a plea to "stop worrying about the problems of education . . . and let teachers and students get on with their lives." Although we are still "serfs on the assembly line" as our current system is set up, teachers and students *are* education. Everything else is superfluous. Take away the buildings, the buses, and so forth, and imagine a group of students with books and a teacher, sitting under a tree on a hilltop outside a small village. Do you or do you not have a school? Yes. Take away the books. Do you still have a school? Yes. Now take away the teacher. Do you still have a school? No!

It could be argued that a teacher without students is also not a school. But, strictly speaking, this is not equally true. A teacher without students is merely a poor teacher—in both senses of the adjective. For example, a restaurant that has no customers at the moment is still a restaurant, albeit not a very successful one. However, does a series of customers all grouped together constitute a restaurant?

It should be obvious that no matter what new programs are implemented, unless they improve things for teachers, they will not improve things for students. Once we remember and hold onto this simple fact, we will have taken the first step out of position: changing our attitude.

Attitude: Defining Our Personal Power

M. Scott Peck retells an old story called "The Rabbi's Gift" in *A Second Helping of Chicken Soup for the Soul* (Canfield & Hansen, 1995). Here is an abridged version:

> An old monastery sat, forgotten and nearly deserted, in a beautiful woods outside a small town. A rabbi kept a hermitage in the same woods, and one day, in desperation, the abbot visited the rabbi to ask his advice about how to save the failing monastery.
>
> The rabbi commiserated with the abbot regarding people's declining interest in matters of faith. "I am sorry," said the rabbi, "I have no advice to give. The only thing I can tell you is that the Messiah is one of you." The disheartened abbot returned to his monks with only that cryptic message.
>
> "What did the rabbi mean?" wondered the monks. "Could he have meant brother Thomas . . . brother Phillip . . . me?" They

began to treat each other with extraordinary respect on the off-chance that one among them might be the Messiah. And on the off, off-chance that each monk himself might be the Messiah, they began to treat *themselves* with extraordinary respect.

Gradually, a change transformed the monastery and the townspeople began to visit regularly once again. The monks' new attitude had created an aura that radiated outward, attracting all and creating a vibrant center of light and spirituality. (pp. 56-59)

A sense of self, of importance, direction, purpose, sufficiency, competence, strength, groundedness, even entrepreneurship —these are all characteristics of personal power. Gatto (1995) writes, "The first thing a teacher has to be is a whole person because teachers teach who they are" (p. 5). A teacher's personal power is not just "nice," it is essential for a whole human being, especially if that human being is expected to nurture the same trait in students. To Goethe has been attributed the sentiment that if you treat someone as though he were already what he ought to be and could be, that is who he will become. This is not news for teachers, who apply it to their students, but not to themselves.

Positive Practices: Applying Them to Ourselves

What's good for students can be good for teachers, too. How many times have you helped students recall good things that they have done or reminded them of their strengths or potential? When was the last time you did this for yourself?

Consultant Connie Muther travels around the world working with teachers. Connie's workshops focus in part on motivational issues: preventing burnout and revealing or nurturing greatness in teachers. Connie likes to ask teachers to tell her about a success they've had. When they've done so, they often tell Connie that no one has ever asked them that before. We may not be asked, but we can ask ourselves. What could it hurt to keep a journal of successes, things that "clicked," new areas of expertise gained? There are times when such a journal could make excellent reading!

What teacher doesn't try to help students recognize their personal areas of expertise and interest? Again, it can help teachers to focus on *their own*. Of course, we don't forget these things about ourselves, but we do tend to crowd them out with so many have-to's and shoulds that they lose their luster. Teachers are becoming re-sponsible for knowledge and certification in ever-increasing areas: teaching English as a second language, teaching awareness of other cultures, teaching students with emotional and behavioral prob-lems and physical and mental impairments. It's easy to bury one's own personal interests and strengths. But these are our greatest as-sets—the way we "add value" to what we do. They bear digging out because they keep us going, give us passion, energy, drive, respect —attitude.

How many teachers display student work? How many display their own degrees, credentials, certificates, awards? Don't adminis-trators have theirs on the wall? Doctors, lawyers, CPAs? Aren't teachers supposed to promote education and achievement? Why not their own? Some people might be amazed by what one must do to become a teacher; it could be good for teachers to remember what they've accomplished.

Don't teachers often try to connect their students with those in another class or school or country or Web site? Why do so? Do we give ourselves the same experiences? Connecting with other teach-ers not from one's school site can boost morale and increase self-respect. Teachers in other districts, states, age groups, demograph-ics, and fields (including private practice, like performing arts teach-ers and athletics coaches) provide access to the bigger picture, give us ideas, boost morale.

Attending international conferences of educators, reading pro-fessional journals, or enrolling in graduate school may offer teachers a more relaxed, respectful, and intellectually stimulating atmos-phere than their daily experiences afford and will combat isolation. Teachers have all kinds of good ideas for promoting self-respect, self-esteem, and morale in other people. Remember the oxygen mask principle: Helping others with their masks first means you won't be around to do anything else once you've passed out from holding your breath.

Teacher Culture: Understanding and Overcoming Taboos and Self-Destructive Behaviors

Whatever our current personal focus—whether we're viewing this year's "cutting-edge" program with a sense of deja vu, taking part in some new project that seems to be making a difference (see

Chapters 1 and 3), or just trying to survive—this is the most stress-filled time ever to be a teacher, a time of constant battle between what needs to be done and what's required. Redefining ourselves will, at first, add to this stress because we will be working against the weight of the old system. However, as our self-induced increase in personal power makes us stronger, healthier, more "whole," we will find stress levels lowering.

As our collective change begins to affect the system itself, we can expect another wave of stress, but we will be equipped to handle it, and this will be the system's stress, not ours directly. Eventually, under a new paradigm system, or network of mini-systems, we will be amazed by what feels like a lack of stress.

The stress of the old system is fatiguing, demoralizing, and unhealthy because it is incessant, ever-increasing, and largely uncontrollable and unrewarded. This type of stress is sometimes termed *distress* (because it is unhealthy) in contrast with *eustress* (which is good for you). For example, veteran teachers cite increases in certification requirements, curricular expectations, and numbers of students "at risk" or with special needs. Often accompanying these increases are lower budgets, fewer materials and enrichment programs, and (reportedly) declining student achievement—formerly one of teachers' greatest rewards. Although financial rewards may have increased somewhat, these are not tied to teachers' performance under stress, merely to the length of their endurance of it.

Normal stress (eustress) ebbs and flows. It does not erode personal worth or energy; on the contrary, it can increase one's feeling of worth and energy because it consists of healthy challenges—those that can be controlled or directed and that have an attainable end point, reward, or payoff. One experiences a sense of achievement, increased capability, growth, and accomplishment under this type of stress. Eustress uplifts rather than weighs down.

Teacher taboos refer to things we just don't discuss. For example, no one ever really discusses the current stresses of being a teacher or how best to cope with them, let alone how to work toward their elimination. During teacher preparation, perhaps instructors have been out of the classroom more than 5 or 6 years—too long to fully understand what's going on today. Perhaps new recruits are too eager, enthusiastic, or idealistic to readily attend such a discussion. Whatever the reasons, the omission of such vital topics during preparation can later render invalid nearly all that *was* discussed.

Once we are actually in the classroom, the current pervasive teacher culture perpetuates our silence regarding topics vital to both our health and our ability to redefine our position. Like those who marry the spouse of their dreams only to learn much later of that spouse's addiction to drugs or alcohol, we are well into our new teaching relationship before we begin to add up the dozens of little danger signals indicative that something more may be amiss than just the difference between reality and dreams. And we are far deeper still before we understand (if we ever do) the addictive nature of the systemic behaviors enveloping us and our codependent part in enabling them to continue.

For spouses in dysfunctional relationships there are doctors, counselors, and friends who can eventually point the way toward support groups and healthier relationships. For teachers, at present, there is no such support network. It is up to us to create one. Teachers need something akin to their own 12-step program to fully recover from working within a system that defines them as less than whole, personally powerful people.

There is a culture of powerlessness among teachers that complements their position. Teachers complain, to be sure, like everyone else, but mostly to each other and rarely to anyone who can make a difference. And there's a great deal that teachers never discuss, hundreds of small, daily stresses that everyone simply takes for granted. This hurts teachers. It ultimately also has to hurt students and society.

The hierarchical and bureaucratic nature of the old system fosters the erosion of teacher morale in many ways, a good percentage of those things seemingly insignificant and not worth the hassle of mentioning them (like the fact that teachers almost never have time to go to the restroom!). But taken together, they can and do become overwhelming, creating a culture of powerlessness, a kind of co-dependence—isolating, passive, or reactive behaviors that enable the erosion to continue.

Isolating Behaviors

Teachers' culture of powerlessness stems from a perceived inability to control anything in the larger picture and the contrapuntal desire to maintain some control in at least one small area. Although there are a good many reasons—negative and positive—for wanting to hole up in one's room with the door closed, the result is still isolation, a cornerstone of current teacher culture. Those who are divided are more easily conquered, subdued, controlled, and intimidated.

Teachers acquiesce to being isolated by grade level; materials, tests, and paperwork can make cross-grade teaming difficult or risky. The opportunities lost are not just students' but teachers' too. Teachers in the United States are isolated by having less planning time than other countries afford their educators. Teachers rarely see each other teach.

When things are not going as well as we'd like, we are all too willing to believe that the problem is in ourselves, that we are somehow inadequate. And, like the codependent spouse, we often get lots of help with this attitude from an administration—and a public —who are all too willing to place the blame on us, leading to shame, guilt, and further isolation. We withdraw inward, work harder, accept more stress, and see fewer ways out—all behaviors that have been considered almost heroic by the old society we grew up in. New paradigm companies install gyms, sponsor employee support groups, and tell employees to take time for a personal life, because they see employees as a resource to be cultivated, not controlled.

PASSIVE BEHAVIORS

Another manifestation of powerlessness is the inability to make decisions or form opinions, to claim a voice. We "can't really say" if this program or those materials ought to be replaced because we "don't know what else is available." We don't think about whether the consultant who presented our inservice is an effective teacher because we "don't know that much" about the subject she taught us. (That in itself should be a clue.) We don't want to evaluate our district administration because we "don't really know exactly" what they do. We'd never let students get away with this type of waffling.

Patricia Wasley (1994, p. 39) studied "Kathryn," a veteran teacher who transferred to a less bureaucratic school. Used to a highly structured, controlling system, she felt overwhelmed: "At the pit of my stomach was the fear that I wasn't smart enough, that I didn't know enough to make these decisions. . . . Because these decisions had always been made for me, somehow I doubted my own abilities." (It should come as no surprise that she also didn't trust her students' abilities.)

Another passive behavior is fear of speaking in public or in front of other teachers. Many teachers claim that they have "no trouble speaking to 30 children" but become petrified in front of a few adults. Old paradigm hierarchical systems create a "pecking order," and the very instant we buy into a pecking order we become someone else's lunch. Teachers who accept a position at the bottom of the chain of command are everybody's lunch. Such teachers fear speaking before other adults because they perceive those adults as more powerful than they—just as they in turn perceive children as less powerful. Kathryn (above) also stated, "It embarrasses me now, but I didn't always believe my students could handle sophisticated work" (Wasley, 1994, p. 38).

When teachers do find their public voice, it is often accompanied by apologies. How many times have we heard a teacher, speaking to a group, say something on the order of "I'm a terrible speller" or "My math isn't too great." Such professed ineptitude is a passive behavior. The person is saying, "I'm really not very good at doing the things necessary to my field."

Do people really sit in college classrooms thinking, "I'm not much good at anything, so I guess I'll become a teacher"? If not, then this self-image has to come, at least in part, from teaching. Because women teachers outnumber men by 2.5 to 1 (National Center for Education Statistics, 1994), it also stems from women's issues like submission to authority, "lesser" competence, dependence, lack of autonomy. There tends to be a higher percentage of women teachers at the elementary level along with generally lower public respect for the level of job skills required; the problem may be more prevalent there. The solution, of course, is to get out of the habit of putting ourselves down and avoiding the respectful rendering of our opinions. If our students put themselves down, we try to help them stop.

REACTIVE BEHAVIORS

Two typical reactive behaviors are "pearl diving" and backroom blustering. Take, for example, staff development. How often have you had to attend a staff development session that in no way pertained to your work? That was about something you already knew? That promised something you wanted but was so poorly organized that you got little from it? Was interesting "enough," had parts you could use, but didn't warrant the time it took? Was scheduled for the day before school began? What did you do about it?

One reactive behavior to such disrespectful, time-wasting, and poor pedagogical practices is pearl diving, probing the depths to find something—anything—good to say about the staff development and then raising one's hand to share this pearl. Doing this could mean we really did like the presentation and are just being enthusiastic, but chances are good that truer opinions will come out in the parking lot. Perhaps it's simply a teaching habit—finding something to praise in every presentation (teachers habitually "like the way you. . . .")—or it could be just brown-nosing.

Another reaction is backroom blustering: complaining to everyone who can't do anything about it. This lets off a certain amount of "steam" without risking confrontation, but it changes nothing. Some people actually complain as well to people who could or might do something. This is known as "getting out of line."

Adult humans, according to Wood and Thompson (1993), learn in ways and for reasons far more similar to young humans than would be apparent from most staff development programs. Teachers learn when learning is perceived as realistic, important, personally and professionally relevant; free of fear, threat, attacks on competence; inclusive of feedback, concrete experiences, and group work; structured to build on diverse personal prior knowledge and experience; and followed up with coaching and transfer in daily practice. Yet Linda Darling-Hammond and Milbrey W. McLaughlin (1995) report that such practices are far from being the norm in staff development programs.

Instead, we sit in lectures where we are told never to lecture. Our attendance is *required* in workshops on student choice. We are almost never asked if we already know what's about to be presented, and even more rarely excused from repetitious training or offered differentiated, advanced, or independent study. Unfortunately, we seldom communicate objections about the quality of teaching we receive. To change our position as teachers will require paying attention to and evaluating such teaching style, content, and relevance. Marshall McLuhan's "The medium is the message" (1964) is apt here.

If, for example, the message is ostensibly to give children concrete experiences relevant to their lives, and the medium for conveying this message to teachers is neither relevant nor particularly concrete, then the real message is that the presenter or the administration does not understand the concepts they are trying to convey. If they don't understand the concepts, they will not know what to look for when they visit our classrooms for follow-up. We could implement exactly what they're talking about (assuming we *do* understand the concepts) and still get into trouble. Therefore, implementation is not our immediate concern; communication and information are what counts.

Unquestioning acceptance is a reactive behavior. When the phone company installs phones in our homes, we decide on the placement and features of the phone. If we put a phone in our child's room, we ask the child for input. If we work for a professional firm and a new in-house phone system is being installed, a company memo or meeting invites employee input on optimally efficient placement and features. Chances are good that teachers who actually have a phone by the year 2000 will be so grateful that it'll never occur to them that they had less input than children in the process of getting it.

Another example occurs when it's midmorning and our elementary class is really getting into the work at hand, things are clicking, we're glad for the lack of interruptions, and suddenly faces appear at our door. Someone from the office is escorting a new student to class. The student speaks no English. There is no accompanying academic record, just instructions as to the correct bus and lunch and when to send the child to the school nurse for unspecified medication. We smile, find a seat for the child, and never question the educational and personal ramifications to the child, to the class, to us. If it's easier for the office to process a new student after classes are already in session, then what does this say about our school's true priorities? Certainly we must all be flexible, but there is a big difference between flexibility and diffidence.

Jane M. Healy gave yet another example in her *Endangered Minds* (1990): "Can they really pass the test? That's a difficult concept.... Of course, it's ridiculous, and the math objectives are almost as unrealistic.... The teachers have objected, but nobody seems to listen. Hey, I can't afford to lose my job!" (p. 270). Obviously, tenure does not equal security to this teacher.

Patronizing treatment and a sense of powerlessness can so pervade the details of daily work that teachers pay little attention to it. We should. Its effects are debilitating, demoralizing, and cumulative; that is, the more we accept it, the more we're willing to put up with. Parents, students, and the public notice it, even comment on and question it, but eventually it colors what they think we're *supposed* to put up with. Keeping silent and trying to comply with the impossible and the educationally unsound may help us survive the moment, but ultimately, it's very unhealthy for us and our students. We must find ways to communicate—and be heard—as equals.

A very good teacher explained her method for "getting what I want without even seeming to ask for it." This is manipulation, not communication; it is reactive to the constraints of the current system, energy expended in evasion tactics and moment-to-moment survival. Passive, isolating, and reactive behaviors not only harm teachers and students, they are enabling to the system. They allow it to continue intact, thus maintaining our current position as teachers-serfs.

The myriad interruptions teachers and students face—from new students who don't show up at the beginning of the day or the period to blaring loudspeakers and clanging factory bells—show at the very least a lack of thought or understanding and, at the very most, a lack of respect. They may be based on fiscal considerations, paperwork or communications difficulties, time constraints, habit, or simply matters of convenience. The reasons are rarely educational in nature.

To stop being passive is not to start being aggressive (another reactive behavior) but to be *assertive*, to find firm but positive ways to communicate what contributes to and what detracts from our work of educating students. This is the beginning of personal power: communicating about the bigger picture and its implications rather than just trying to comply. We must learn to make our communications open, honest (though tactful), assertive, and peer based, not fear based. Remember Deming's dictum about driving fear out of the workplace. We must examine what it is that teachers are afraid of and replace fear with self-confidence and self-respect.

"What learning theories support this concept?" "Where can I get further information?" "Can you demonstrate how you think this will work?" "What helped you decide on this program?" "It's better for everyone if a new student can arrive at the beginning of the day or period. Is there a way we can make this work?" "This policy doesn't seem to support learning efficiently. What about . . .?"

It isn't enough to ask such questions alone. Solo flights into assertiveness training leave us at most expendable and at least targetable, robbing us of any credibility we once had. Nor can we yet look to our unions for this type of support. They are still used to pleading cases to a "higher authority" because of their origins as part of the hierarchical bureaucracy. They don't yet understand networks, webs, or personal power; they see all three as a threat to their existence. Vouchers, an opportunity for credentialed teachers to network with each other and bypass administration, are the ultimate union victory, and also the end of its current purpose. Unless or until we can convince unions of a new purpose, help them envision a new role, they will fight anything that threatens the old system still defining them.

Teachers cannot go it alone, nor are there built-in supports. Fortunately, teachers are good at networking. We are constantly borrowing ideas, materials, and support for our classrooms. We just need to start borrowing for ourselves. Remember Goethe: Teachers must ask to be treated as if they already were what they ought to be and could be. What's good for students is good for teachers, too.

We know from our teaching that a lack of morale and respect is both contagious and sufferable, that is, once it starts spreading, we feel there's nothing we can do about it, and once we feel there's nothing we can do about it, we learn to live with whatever it is, creating a vicious cycle. Eleanor Roosevelt is credited with saying, "No one can make you feel inferior without your own consent." We must withdraw our consent. Or, as John Robbins points out in *Reclaiming Our Health* (1996), the best way to get someone off a power pedestal is to get up off your knees.

Professional, Public Image: Changing Ours

A great deal of this book is devoted to personal worldview and attitude because they are the key to everything. As we embrace true change, as we redefine ourselves and our role, our public image will begin to change also. In case you're harboring the mistaken impression that our public image is untarnished, turn for a moment to film. In recent years, *Dead Poets' Society, Mr. Holland's Opus*, and *Stand and Deliver* have been considered excellent films and tributes to teachers. Yet in the first two, the teachers lost their jobs and in the third, the teacher nearly died. Is this what popular culture considers a good teacher: one we got rid of?

We need to think of both the image that we convey to the public and the contribution our image makes to that of teachers in general. Akin to having our diplomas on the wall and a computer at home is having a career plan, an overall scheme of what we would like to have done in the next 3, 5, and 10 years. There is no longer any field one can enter thinking, "I can do this until I retire." Those days were part of the old reality. Where can we go as teachers? That is part of what we must define through our personal new worldview and our professional networks, journals, and international conferences.

A simpler part of our image has to do with keeping a sports jacket handy for meetings and equipping our restrooms with clothes hooks, hair dryers, and other amenities for repairs and touch-ups—like real people with real jobs. It deals with bigger issues like computer-generated, spell-checked newsletters, parent letters, and homework—all free of mechanical and grammatical errors. Susan Kovalik (1995) says, "Teachers can't teach what they can't do!" (Side 1). Why send children for literacy skills to a teacher who doesn't have any?

When installing a computerized bookkeeping system for a small printing and marketing firm, I was asked to train the young bookkeeper. One of her first tasks was to send a letter to clients and vendors explaining that we would be conducting an internal audit and requesting their assistance on a questionnaire that would accompany the next monthly statement. The copy she wrote for duplication and mailing contained grammatical errors and obvious typos and was not centered on the page. I asked her to put herself in the place of a customer receiving such an unprofessional letter from a firm in the business of printing and advertising. She did, and she changed the letter.

This young woman had good intentions but hadn't been thinking about image. It wasn't her company. She wasn't committed to doing the best quality work, just to getting by. She had nothing to lose except a low-paying job that she didn't like that much anyway. Regardless of what she wrote, this was the message her original letter conveyed by the *way* it was written.

We cannot afford to give handwritten assignments in a world run on computers. We cannot afford to be nonreaders and nonwriters when our national educational focus is on literacy. We cannot afford to let people hear us butcher the English language or make up words like "ekcetera," "districk," "adjetive," or "picher." Nor can we afford to make light or flippant comments about our academic short-comings as though humility excused rigor. For example, while teaching middle school humanities, I sat, aghast, in a parent conference as my math-science partner recounted how he had flunked Algebra 1 when he was in junior high. I'm sure the parent with whom we were meeting was overjoyed to have this man teaching algebra to her gifted son. I've heard from more teachers than I care to count how poor they are at spelling or math. Such comments are intended to "break the ice," be "humble," to show that we (they reflect on all teachers) know how it feels to make mistakes. In fact, they merely feed public perceptions like "Those who can, do. Those who can't, teach."

Would you hire a tax consultant who told you she'd been penalized by the IRS for errors in filing her own return? Would the fact that she knows how it feels to mess up and get audited increase your confidence in her ability to file your return? Would you hire a building contractor whose own house fell down? (I can give you an address . . .)

New Teacher Traits: Three Experts' Definitions

John Taylor Gatto (former New York State Teacher of the Year, and a writer and speaker), Michael Fullan (Dean, Faculty of Education, University of Toronto, author and speaker), and Peter Senge (Director, Systems Thinking and Organizational Learning, Sloan School of Management, MIT) all give us glimpses into who we must become if our teaching is to remain valuable enough to afford us students. As summarized and paraphrased below, Gatto (1995) and Fullan (1993) describe what the new teacher must be, whereas Senge (1990) describes the personal mastery needed for continual growth and learning.

Gatto:

1. Whole, and recognizably independent
2. Willing to reject inferior books, materials, and tests, and able to show why
3. Autonomous regarding curriculum and sequencing, and public enough to attract students who are a "match"
4. An independent speaker, not a transmitter of others' words

5. Knowledgeable of self and of the limits and dangers of institutions

Fullan:

1. Actively, visibly committed to making a difference for children
2. Having a deep and substantial personal knowledge of pedagogy
3. Cognizant of the links among school issues, education policy, and societal development
4. Having independent personal purpose and vision; working interactively, collaboratively
5. Working in new structures and joining wider networks
6. Developing the habits and skills of continuous inquiry and learning
7. Immersed in the change process

Senge:

1. Continually clarifying what's important
2. Continually learning to see current reality more clearly
3. Having a strong sense of purpose or mission
4. Learning to work with change forces, not resist them
5. Deeply inquisitive
6. With a self-image of uniqueness, yet connected to others and to life itself
7. Consciously part of a larger creative process
8. Living in a continual learning mode
9. Acutely aware of their ignorance, their growth areas
10. Deeply self-confident

We need to not only develop and improve these traits but also polish our interpersonal communication with all ages, including our writing, computing, and public-speaking skills. We must use our newly developing attitude of personal power; our self-image at the *core* of the educational web, not the bottom of its hierarchy; and our growing self-respect and self-affirming behaviors to dispel any doubts that we will eventually embody all these traits and skills. At the same time, we must support and encourage each other in our efforts.

Greatness: Finding It in Ourselves

Despite all our efforts and aspirations, it's easy these days to feel incapable or insufficiently prepared. Look at the demands being placed on teachers and ask yourself, What human being could possibly meet all of them? Teachers cannot repair society or assume the responsibilities others are unwilling or unable to face. However, we can, all of us, provide leadership toward the new emerging society by speaking up for what we know works.

No program or method—new or old—will work for every teacher and every student. What works for us will not work for everyone, but the point is that it does work for us. It's becoming well accepted that students learn in different ways, through different intelligences. The point is to match students with similar teachers through choice (new-paradigm customization and individual power) and stop trying to force everyone into old-paradigm uniformity.

From her work in finding and interviewing great teachers, consultant Connie Muther (personal communication, September 4, 1996) draws three common characteristics. Great teachers

1. Love their work—their bond with the kids, their subject area, the teaching itself
2. Have a passion or mission that drives them
3. Can't be copied, nor would we want to copy them

The last point is extremely important, because greatness comes from the personal interests and expertise we talked about earlier (pp. 19-20). Because these teachers have given themselves an outlet for their own passions, rather than stifling themselves in compliance, their personal greatness has had a chance to shine through.

Connie tells the story of Jack Musgrave of Warsaw, Indiana, a high school writing teacher recommended to Connie by his assistant superintendent. When she first observed Jack, Connie had been interviewing great teachers (as recommended by their administration and peers) for 4 years and in several countries. She felt confident that she knew what to look for.

On entering Jack's room, she found the walls completely bare, the students seated but in total disorder, and the teacher invisible. Her gut instinct was to leave, which she did after a few minutes. However, in talking with other teachers at that school, she was asked repeatedly whether she had been to Jack's room. If she was interviewing great teachers, she had to interview Jack. "Why?" she finally asked. The answer: Because Jack gets students to turn out incredible work.

It was near the end of the period when Connie found Jack, seated on a chair with casters and huddled with a couple of students in one corner of his classroom, the rest of the class in boisterous disarray. He indicated he could talk with her after the bell and, still seated, wheeled his chair toward the front of the room. She said that moment reminded her of an E. F. Hutton commercial: Talking stopped and attention riveted on him as he gave the next day's assignment.

After class, Jack explained that he conferenced individually with each student every day. If the other students, tired of sitting in classes all day, got a little rowdy while waiting, it didn't bother him so long as they did not get out of hand. The important thing was not how loudly they discussed their writing topic (or anything else), when they wrote, nor what else they did while waiting for him. The important thing was how they wrote, their finished writing product. He expected—and got—their very best writing. Every day.

Such a teacher would be condemned by those administrators who evaluate teachers and programs on 5-minute walk-throughs looking for displays of student work and neat, orderly seating arrangements. They would be wrong. And we need to defend every teacher who would be judged by those who value decorated walls, familiar activities, and even test scores over individual excellence.

We need to share our successes and those of others through journals, networking, and mutual promotion. And we must support each other when we make mistakes, rather than allowing withdrawal into isolation. We need to reclaim the right to decide what is good teaching and the responsibility to let our students and their work judge our accuracy.

In order to do this, we'll need to do our homework. We'll need to read, to study, and to risk, to require time and support for personally relevant learning and growth, time that should count as independent study, replacing some staff development. If our district needs or wants particular staff development and not enough teachers are taking such courses, the district should offer incentives rather than requiring everyone to sit through the same thing no matter what —the model of poor pedagogical practice.

As we begin to network and support each other, as we find our voices and begin to assert ourselves, as we require that respect accompany responsibility, we will make mistakes. Mistakes are embarrassing only to egos; to the brain they are an integral part of the learning process. A baby would never learn to walk if she or he didn't first fall down repeatedly. Mistakes tell learners what to adjust. "Failure is an opportunity for learning" (Senge, 1990, p. 154). "A mistake is an event, the full benefit of which has not yet been turned to your advantage" (Ed Land, founder of Polaroid, in Senge, 1990, p. 154). We must learn from our mistakes, forgive those who don't want to give us a second chance, seek and accept support from our colleagues, and keep going.

Greatness is as unique as each individual. We tell our students that. Now we must tell ourselves that. We cannot begin to believe in the potential of every student until we believe in the potential of every teacher.

3

Becoming the New Teacher

We won't get different schools from the same old
teachers any more than we'll get a different piece of cake
from the same old recipe. . . . If schools are to break from
20th century school tradition, if schools are to be more
successful than our familiar ones, I suspect the key will
reside in a new kind of person to lead the class, not in
technology or fancy routines. . . . Most restructuring
schemes floating around do not reach into the heart of the
problem: We need to reinvent the teacher. We need
teachers we never had.

JOHN TAYLOR GATTO, 1995, PP. 2-3

In Chapter 2, we discussed the personal change in attitude we
need to make in order to shift out of our old position and align
ourselves with our culture's new worldview, the new paradigm
—that is, to redefine teaching. When we begin to make that personal
change, it will naturally affect how we teach. We need to consciously
expand that positive personal influence into our practice in order to
complete our redefinition, to become, if you will, a New Teacher.

Redefining Our Approach

First, let's look at a list of common teaching beliefs. (If there are
friends of yours among them, prepare your good-byes.) We should

be able to relate why each belief belongs to the old paradigm and conflicts with current research and the new worldview.

Old Beliefs

1. We have the power to be responsible for others' learning.
2. Some learners come to us with less experience or knowledge than others.
3. If a concept is too difficult for certain learners, they will get nothing from working on it.
4. Disorder or confusion in a group of learners is a warning that they are not learning and need further clarification.
5. Breaking things down into a logical series of steps aids learning.
6. Simplifying material makes learning easier.
7. Reteaching helps learners who did not understand the first time.
8. Making sure everyone understands before moving on is important.
9. Labeling behaviors and learning difficulties helps us determine specific methods of working with learners who have them.
10. A learner's personal hardships will prevent learning.
11. The number of minutes we spend teaching, as opposed to other activities, is important.
12. Covering required material is important.
13. Sticking to the lesson plan is important.
14. Our job is to try to make learning easy and fun.
15. What learners can do as a result of our help is difficult to assess or control, and should have nothing to do with our pay or continued employment.

As you can see, there is much we must "unlearn" before we can define and embody a new way of being a teacher. An ancient Zen story has become popular as a way to describe this "unlearning" process:

There was a well-educated and respected man who decided to add to his wealth of knowledge by studying with a Zen master. When he arrived, he stated his name, his purpose, and his degrees. The master asked if he would have tea. He agreed, and they sat at a low table where the master placed a cup in front of the learned man and began to pour the tea.

The master poured and poured and the man watched with increasing agitation as the tea approached the rim of the cup. When it overflowed, the man lost his temper and exclaimed, "Stop! Can't you see the cup is full?" The master calmly set the teapot down and answered, "If you would learn something new, first you must empty your cup."

Learners (including teachers) are responsible for their own learning; no one can assume power over someone else's life. (It's difficult enough trying to assume power over our own!) All learners bring their unique experiences to learning; the differences are measurable more in type than in quantity. Based on their experiences, all learners will take what they are ready for from each given situation, no less and no more; better than belaboring or repeating is cycling back over key concepts at a later date and/or transferring their application to a different learning modality or subject area.

Disorder and confusion are natural steps in the learning process; they lead to the questions that lead to learning. However, learning is not a linear, sequential process, and learners do not all learn the same content from the same questions. Nor do we learn things in isolation, "simplified" out of context of their whole.

Labels may simply distance the facilitator by depersonalizing rather than individualizing the learner. The brain tends to retain the emotional "charge" that first accompanied a learning, whether it was a label or a threatening environment, and to "call up" that feeling in later life when the learning is used. For this reason, it helps if learning environments feel safe; however, masses of people have learned during war and other terrifying or stressful times, so the question is more one of personal relevance and purpose. If there's something we really want, and learning will get it for us, we will learn. And learning is occurring at all times; the only question is "Which learning?"

We need to teach students how to acquire information in better and better ways and how to turn this information into knowledge that has value. This process, framed in ways that are personally relevant to students, is key and takes precedence over content and pre-established lesson plans. Learning is naturally fun and rewarding, though not always easy. Our approach must facilitate, not get in the way of, this natural process.

And finally, a true professional's status, pay, and ability to find clients depends on previously satisfied and successful clients. How long we're willing to work for a particular employer should have nothing to do with our pay. How many clients we have should not be a political football, but an educational and reputational decision.

Even if we cannot yet completely understand or agree with the reasons why none of the old beliefs is any longer "true," we must agree to at least let go *enough* to temporarily suspend judgment as we try something new.

Building New Beliefs

Remembering Gatto's statement, "Teachers teach who they are" (1995, p. 6), we can begin to build new beliefs and practices. Seeing things from a newly empowered and more holistic view, we will naturally begin using a more experiential, empowered approach. We will interweave formerly separate subjects within hands-on tasks created by and relevant or important to both ourselves and our students. We will facilitate students' own construction of knowledge, rather than trying to be the source of their knowledge and the maker of their decisions, just as we are reclaiming both these functions in our own lives. We will remember to trust ourselves and, therefore, we can begin to truly trust our students.

We are aware that the sum of all human knowledge is now said to double in less than 10 years. The Police sang about "too much information"; Gore wrote that information can become a kind of pollution. In the Information-Age world filled with knowledge-based, "smart" products and value-added services that both promote and require continual learning, we understand that teachers simply cannot continue trying to deliver content. Knowing how to analyze floods of information, then synthesize and apply that which is individually useful (or potentially marketable to others) has become the most important type of learning—for our students, and for ourselves—and we will apply our new understanding of knowledge to our teaching.

Redefining Our Practice

> It's quite a responsibility to decide what you're going to teach, to decide what the kids should learn. You're grappling with the real nitty-gritty: What do we want kids to get out of school? What's important here? How do we do that? ("Kathryn" in Wasley, 1994, p. 39)

Okay, so we understand our situation and where we need to go. We're working on a new, more positive and powerful self-image. We're developing the traits and skills of the New Teacher. And now, it's Monday morning. What do we *do*?

Research Guidelines: Using Three Criteria for Optimal Learning

A 1995 qualitative research survey (mine) into what the fields of education, business, the performing arts, the new physics, and brain research considered best pedagogical practice yielded several common characteristics. The three most often emphasized were that learning must be personal, natural, and cyclical (see Figure 3.1).

Under each of these primary categories it's possible to group the other most emphasized descriptors:

Learning occurs best when it is

PERSONAL:

Experiential—based on learner's own experience

Learner relevant—significantly related to learner's world

Learner directed—imbued with learner choices

Starts wherever the learner is—neither too difficult nor too easy

Allows work with others

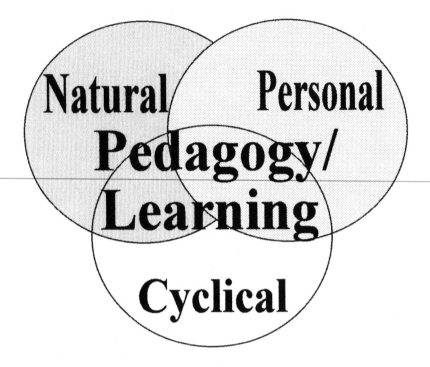

Qualitative research done in 1995 into learning theories in education, staff development research and theory, creativity theory, and performing arts and athletics practice, plus current business theory, new science theory, and future theories, yielded a number of common principles regarding learning, which fall into the three main categories above.

Figure 3.1. Three Criteria for Optimal Learning

NATURAL:
> Real-world based—connects to the world outside the class-room
>
> Brain compatible
>
> Multi-intelligence based
>
> Without force or fear
>
> Context (not content) and process oriented
>
> Thematic and integrated (not subject centered)

CYCLICAL (NONLINEAR):
    Continual (seen as both constant and lifelong)
    Takes order through disorder to higher order
    Builds on prior knowledge
    Transfers to other situations and returns, enriched, to the original

Monday Morning Techniques: Theme Cycle

A good way to become comfortable with our new beliefs and practices is the theme cycle. Theme cycles continually build on prior knowledge, tailor study to personal needs and interests, and follow a natural learning pattern while they empower learners and teachers. Places for both pre- and postassessments are built in. You can see the theme cycle spiral back at a higher level as you read the standard questions formatting it. Just fill in the blank with your concept or topic.

1. What do you already know about _____?
2. What do you want to know about _____?
3. How will you find out?
4. How will you report back?
5. What did you learn? (Now what do you know?)
6. What new questions did your learning raise? (Now what do you want to know?)
7. How will you answer these?

Have students record everyone's answers on butcher paper (so you can save it) or on the board (if you're doing it in 1 day). You can also record responses on an overhead, especially if the children are too young to print their own responses.

A theme cycle can be as specific or as open-ended as suits your purpose. Say at 9:55 the office announces over the loudspeaker that the 10:00 assembly will be delayed by half an hour. You could do a theme cycle about delays, the assembly topic, time, PA systems, and so on.

At the other extreme, a completely open theme cycle is an excellent way to begin the year: "What do you already know?" Kids love filling butcher paper with all their skills and accomplishments. Then ask what they want to learn this year. Around December, pull out the butcher paper to see how you're doing, checking off what you've covered on the "What do you want to learn?" page. Do this again after spring break and assign year-end "personal projects" to complete the odds-and-ends topics appealing to only a few. By year-end, you'll have covered everything the students wanted to learn, giving them direct ownership of the curriculum.

How do we make certain that what the students want to learn is what they will need to learn? During the students' work on their topics (or subtopics within your topic) it's the teacher's job to:

1. Find opportunities for reinforcing basic skills
2. Introduce required curriculum through related topic areas
3. Provide many resources for in-depth investigations

For example, students want to learn about a popular book series or computer game, so we (a) conduct surveys within the class and other classes and predict, calibrate, and graph the results; (b) write to the author, write similar books, or create a new computer game; (c) research historical counterparts for the book series or the computer game; and (d) use book or game contents to do science experiments or research. The possibilities are literally endless. Instead of pushing learning onto students ready-made, we are pulling it from their own interests and abilities. This technique will be discussed in further detail in Chapter 4.

Why Am I Doing This?
Connecting Details in a New Picture

We've discussed the big picture of change, the fundamental reasons why it's time and why it's right. We've explored the major changes we need to make in personal attitude and professional traits. A holistic, systemic approach holds that everything is interrelated and interdependent. The real test of whether we are adopting this paradigm comes in how we handle the details.

All teachers have many methods, techniques, and tools that work extremely well and others that are based on habit or familiarity or previously unquestioned requirements. To cull those that support our new position requires examining every little thing we do or plan and asking ourselves, "Why am I doing this? Do I enjoy it? Do the kids enjoy it? What, exactly, are they learning from it? What's the educational point and which learning theory (theories) and research supports it? Is it part of the old way of thinking, holding me back; can I adapt it to fit my new position?"

Everything we do includes not only our planning, teaching, and homework, but also the ubiquitous structures of our days—from hall duty to attendance—that become almost too obvious to see. Brain research shows us that thoughts form synapses between neural axons and dendrites, and repeated thoughts (e.g., habits) create strong neural pathways—sort of interneural freeways. These are permanent and fall into disuse only when stronger habits supplant them (we build a better freeway). Collateral learning theory tells us that learning never stops. We gather new information and insights. We filter in new information that reinforces old beliefs. Or we simply play existing beliefs over in our minds like cerebral Muzak tape loops. It depends a great deal on whether our environment is personally meaningful (and therefore motivating or stimulating). Kovalik and Olsen (1991) state, "The environment of the school and classroom virtually bristle with messages to students" (p. 8). Which messages learners attend to depends on whether we have reinforced natural learning processes. It depends on whether we have practiced building on prior knowledge (cycling). It depends on how well students can—and how much they care to—focus their attention in a particular area.

EXAMPLE 1

The performing arts and sports are two fields where focused attention and details are critical. Dan Millman (1980), a former University of California world champion gymnast, writes of his mentor:

> One time I finished my best-ever pommel horse routine and walked over happily to take the tape off my wrists. [My mentor] beckoned me and said, "The routine looked satisfactory, but you did a very sloppy job taking the tape off. Remember, every-moment satori" [complete body-mind immersion in every detail of the moment]. (p. 157)

It is this complete focusing of attention, this point "when a person's body or mind is stretched to its limits in a voluntary effort to

accomplish something difficult and worthwhile" that Csikszentmihalyi (1990) calls optimal experience or flow (p. 3).

EXAMPLE 2

A group of California educators met to process and promote a
new assessment system. After listening to opening remarks about
the tremendous importance of the work we would be doing for children and their future, we took a short break with refreshments.
Food was served on styrofoam; drinks were served in bottles or
cans. No recycling containers were provided and no one (else) asked
for any. Hundreds of plastic plates and cups and utensils joined
scores of cans and bottles in garbage bound for landfills. Our words
said we are very concerned about children and their future. Our actions said we weren't too concerned. *We either "get it" and everything
changes, or we talk about it and nothing changes.*

When we engage in a lot of meaningless activities during our
day, then a lot of our learning (and our students') is also meaningless. It's the little things that add up to a way of learning for life.
When we drive down a familiar highway in light traffic, we may
startle ourselves by realizing that we don't remember passing a
particular landmark. "Where" were we as we were driving past it?
"Who" was driving? People often work this way, too, out of familiarity with the task or in withdrawal from stress.

It's a very different story when our highway is congested and
conditions are treacherous. We switch to "survival" mode and every
instinct, all our senses are sharp, alert. As teachers, we're in that
mode right now in public education, or we need to be. We need to
look at everything as though we are visitors from another field (or
another planet!). Questioning the little things can reveal much that
we should change and much that we should strengthen and keep.

STORYTIME

Many years ago, my neighbors told me this story of a newlywed
couple:

A young bride was eager to impress and please her new husband
with a delicious meal on the weekend. She bought a roast and
prepared it by cutting it in half, adding various seasonings and

cooking it, all according to a family recipe. Her husband loved it, but had one question: "Honey, why did you cut the roast in half before cooking it?"

After some thought, she could reply only, "That was the way my mother taught me to prepare a roast." They decided, for fun, to call her mother and find out whether this trick of cutting the roast in half before seasoning added special flavor.

Her mother's reply: "I'm not sure. That's the way my mother taught me."

Now intrigued, they phoned the grandmother and asked, "Grandma, why does our family recipe call for cutting a roast in half before cooking it?"

Grandma chuckled and replied, "Well, when your grandfather and I were first married, we didn't own a large roasting pan, just two small ones."

An interesting theme cycle could be to explore with students why we do some of the things we do and how to eliminate, streamline, delegate, or enhance these activities. Applying learning theories and research to something simple, like taking attendance and lunch count, and seeing the interdependent learning inherent in all school activities is a new-paradigm approach to curriculum, employing basic skills like mathematical algorithms but far more personally relevant and natural than their isolated, abstract study.

Putting elementary students in charge of attendance and lunch count and giving them 10 minutes each morning to take care of this and other business makes a daily detail into a learning opportunity. With table groups, each table leader can take attendance and lunch count, then record them in a central location. One student or the whole class can total them, keep weekly records to graph, find differences, percentages, patterns, probabilities, or potential independent variables, depending on the students' level.

Other details will come into bold relief as the noneducational interruptions that they really are. We can then raise awareness, suggest alternatives, discuss them, and network to get them changed. Although bureaucratic systems are good at continuing to cut the roast in half, most people within them would rather use just one pan, once they know "why."

Redefining Our Materials

As New Teachers, we should be able to examine any new re-search, materials package, books, or curriculum and show where and how it supports, extends, or runs contrary to the learning theories we subscribe to and practice. That is, is it natural, cyclical, and personal? Is it adaptable, flexible, easily able to be customized? Or is it one-size-fits-all, based on step-by-step, linear increments, assuming that what was a logical progression for the authors will seem equally logical to all teachers and students?

Example

The district is going to buy a new line of reading books and you have been asked to be on a committee that helps select the particular brand districtwide. First, you could compliment your curriculum director on the wisdom of getting user input before purchasing. (Be careful not to thank! Peers compliment; inferiors are grateful.) You could inquire as to the prices of the various lines, in order to make a fully informed (adult) decision. Also, what schools have used and recommend each brand, what research went into its development, and what learning theories does it support and how?

Are the books personally relevant and important to your students? If the publisher is foreign, check for idiomatic or indigenous expressions (like, "He lit his torch inside the dark barn" or "'Come on, let's have a go at it,' she said") that are particularly difficult in lower grades or for second-language learners.

What is the point of view? If you teach in the city, do the books focus on city or country life? Are the ethnicities represented personally relevant to your students? Are multiple intelligences addressed in any way? Are the books appropriate for both team and individual work and supportive of your overall curriculum? Or are we in effect asking Florida kindergartners to build paper snowmen?

Remembering that we are the teachers, we should not have to accept something that won't work for us. If the district is bent on "one size" and that size doesn't fit us, we could ask that the portion of funding that would have gone to our class (or school) be excluded from the order and given to us to purchase materials on our own. Even when we don't succeed in getting what we need or want, our questions are important—at the very least for our self-respect, and at the most for the seeds of ultimate change that they plant.

Redefining Our Curriculum

The multibillion-dollar textbook and testing industries, the federal government, state governments, districts, and school boards all define curriculum, outcomes, and various kinds of assessments. We should read and regularly refer back to these documents for our grade level(s) because it's strategic to know what's passing as sound educational policy; how it's practical, feasible, supported, funded, and contradicted; how it supports theory, research, and the new paradigm, and how, where, and why we do or do not implement it in our classrooms.

As New Teachers, we should feel competent to discuss any outcomes, objectives, or curricula with anyone, from the people who wrote them to the state superintendent of public instruction, parents, the school custodian, and, most important, students themselves. We should shelve well-thumbed copies of state and district (and even federal) documents, research, and professional books and journals in our classrooms next to our desks (and under our diplomas, etc.). We need to know what we're talking about. We need to continually strengthen our knowledge. In the Information Age, more than ever before, useful knowledge is power. As Don Juan asks Carlos in Castaneda's *The Teachings of don Juan*, "What is the sense in knowing things that are useless?" (1968, p. 24).

Assessment

No human being could cover everything in all the official curricula. Our selections need to be based on our particular students, our own expertise, available resources, and special school or district goals. Unfortunately, the tail often wags the dog here. For example, raising scores on a particular test (in order to publish them in the local newspaper) too often takes precedence among the powers that be over students' learning anything useful (or anything at all). Frank Smith (1995) writes, "Assessment—maintaining pressure on people caught in the system—is the only thing many politicians think of when they take a problem-solving approach to education" (p. 587).

Although there is no pat answer for this common dilemma, we must maintain in our classrooms those programs we have researched, found to produce the greatest learning in the greatest number of students, tailored to our students' particular needs and interests, and infused with our own personal areas of expertise and passion. If we have done all that, then our students should do well on any tests of knowledge, aptitude, and curriculum.

Preassessment

However, all assessment is meaningless unless preassessment was also done. That is, assessments and tests may demonstrate certain knowledge or skills but cannot show how, when, or where these skills were acquired. All teachers preassess. It's how we do it that counts.

Preassessment is often done by instinct. Teachers sense where children are, through behaviors, comments, and work produced by them, often with uncanny accuracy. Unfortunately, teachers are not yet in a position for their word to be sufficient. And, to be sure, there are a very few whose word would come from prejudice or lack of information. Therefore, it's necessary to record preassessments. The record can be a pretest matched to a posttest, a form, or a simple narrative. It's important to use the same format for all students and to make results as easy to compare—both with postassessments and with other students—as possible.

Many teachers have excellent assessments in place that yield information valuable to them, their students, parents, and others. Required assessments of all kinds can take an enormous amount of time and energy (Frank Smith [1995, pp. 586-587] says at least 33%) and still yield nothing that we didn't already know, whereas everything from favored status to tenure can be tied to their completion and results. It's medieval.

Parameters

But that's exactly what we're trying to change, so we need to arm ourselves with the best information possible, put it in writing, and support it with the ideas of the best and most respected minds of our new era. Then we need to relegate useless and time-consuming tasks to the smallest possible frame, delegate them whenever possible to parent volunteers (who will also find them useless and time-consuming and may plead our case for us) or make them into real-life student lessons.

Some useful parameters for checking the content of our curriculum might be:

1. What learning theory, writing, research is it based on?
2. Is it personally relevant to the learners?
3. Is it compatible with natural (brain-based) learning?
4. Where is it cycled? Transferred?
5. From where did the students start?
6. What is the expected outcome?
7. How is it being pre- and postassessed?

Redefining Our Responsibility

Responsibility must be modeled, delegated, and limited. As we move out of our lowly position on the assembly-line model and begin to take our place in an egalitarian web or network, we must begin to make our classrooms more egalitarian. Recalling the recycling example of educators "committed to the future" but sending tons of recyclable materials to landfills, we either get it or we don't. The theory of transfer tells us that real learning is that which can be applied in more than one situation, that in fact the brain requires transfer of applications in order for learning to be complete. As we become empowered, we will transfer that empowerment to our students.

For example, a toddler who discovers how to open and close a door will want to continue to open and close that door—and several others—for a period of time until all possible variations have been exhausted and door opening and closing is a complete concept (or the parent's tolerance is exhausted). It is, no doubt, this same learning principle that led me one afternoon, at the age of 3, to take the labels off every can of food in the cupboard, making mealtime a voyage of discovery for my mother for some time afterward!

Increasing Student Responsibility

The point is, once we begin to experience empowerment, we will begin to transfer it to those around us. The reason *empower* has lost the meaning Freire gave it in *Pedagogy of the Oppressed* (1972) and has become an irritating educational buzzword is that teachers cannot possibly empower students when they themselves are disenfranchised. Claiming our own personal power helps us guide students in claiming theirs, and, incidentally, makes teaching easier all around.

Two "checkpoints" in our efforts to delegate responsibility and make our classrooms more egalitarian are as follows:

1. Never do anything you could have a student do.
2. Never ask a student to do something you are unwilling to do (i.e, that you feel is "beneath" you).

When we delegate responsibility to students, we must trust that they will fulfill it. Undoubtedly, their work will be different from what ours would have been, but that's OK. In some cases, it might even be better! (That's OK, too.) However, we must not accept work that is less than their personal best.

We must let go of the conditioned impulse to give responsibility linearly, in increments. When we give small or meaningless responsibilities first, with the thought that we will let students "earn" more later, we are maintaining our Newtonian beliefs in building blocks and control.

Instead, we can have class meetings about responsibilities. We can have students list, analyze, and categorize all the ones they can think of. We can discuss the meaning of responsibility, then ask the students what they'd be willing to take on. In the process, we've created an interdependent system and destroyed a hierarchy; empowered students and freed ourselves; used writing, public speaking, analysis, categorizing, synthesis, decision making, consensus, teamwork, and probably some math—all in a real, personally relevant, brain-compatible way. We can go to recess.

Limiting Teacher Responsibility

We must know whose responsibility is whose, that is, where ours stops and the learner's begins, and where they overlap. If a student is learning 101 ways to scale the playground fence, our teaching responsibility is to draw out skills and concepts from the student's areas of interests (How high is the fence? How many seconds does it take to get over and back? How could you decrease the time? How do firefighters use these skills?) and to promote growth in the student's social responsibility (What will be the consequences if you keep climbing over the fence? Are you prepared to face those consequences? Why could climbing the fence be dangerous to you? To others? Why is the fence there? What could you do instead?).

Although it is our responsibility to teach, it is the learner's responsibility to learn. If someone is not ready or motivated to learn, we can help prepare or motivate, but we cannot force. Contrary to popular opinion, it is not a teaching responsibility to parent, police, or psychoanalyze. To accept such responsibilities when they are thrust upon us is codependent and reactive behavior that enables a dysfunctional, irresponsible society to remain just that. It's impossible to fulfill all the responsibilities others would like to abdicate. Trying to do so merely keeps us from teaching.

We have a responsibility to all our students, and in an effort to recognize that, the system has been emphasizing students at risk or challenged. We still have a responsibility to so-called average students as well as to students who excel in particular areas or all around. If our average and above-average students become neglected, then our future average and above-average wage earners become endangered, creating an insufficient tax base to support special services for our at-risk and challenged populations. We cannot afford to be so shortsighted.

Businesses today discuss responsibility and marketing regarding suppliers and consumers, both internal and external. Internally, our most important consumers are our students and our most important suppliers are parents. Parents can make completely erroneous assumptions about the lack of stress and expertise required in teaching, about the appropriateness of the current system, or about the rights and responsibilities of their individual children versus the class as a whole. Parents, for the most part, have to assume that there's a good reason for cutting the roast in half because that's the way it was done when they were in school and because they have very little idea what actually goes on in classrooms today. We need to help them understand.

Our external suppliers and customers include society as a whole. Our responsibility is to be cognizant of our part in and contribution to that larger picture and to find our voices. As we have seen, our education system is not the only possible system, nor is it any longer the right one for our times. The point is to accept full responsibility for teaching and for contributing to societal change. Period. That's more than enough.

4

Viewing the New Teacher in Action

Creating Our Information-Age Learning Models

It bears repeating that there is no one right model or program, no single teaching method that is going to fix education, make children literate, or produce a responsible society. The way teachers are teaching is not the problem with education, as we have seen.

However, we have also seen that a paradigm shift is all-inclusive, touching details in our personal and professional lives and wedding them to major concepts about the nature of reality. And because of this, our teaching will shift, too. This shift will occur individually, because of changes within us, not across the board due to changes imposed upon us from above.

The shifts that will produce the greatest gains for students are those that produce the greatest gains for teachers—changes in attitude and self-image, shifts toward entrepreneurship and away from a subservient culture. For example, at a recent math inservice, teachers were being encouraged to accept a variety of methods from students, so long as each method arrived at the desired result. At the same time, the teachers themselves were being encouraged to gradually eschew other methods than the one being presented. The paradoxical nature of the presentation was never discussed—at least not aloud. (See Teacher Culture, Chapter 2.) It must be discussed. It must be displaced.

The successful models of teaching that emerge will be many and varied, like the teachers who create them, and they will be continually changing and improving, like other creations of their era. To create these models, we need to ask ourselves, "What method, what model do I already use with great success? Why does it work? What learning theories and research support it? What else do I need to know about it to make it work even better? Where do I find the information and get practice with feedback? What else would I like to learn about how to successfully improve it with students and promote it with parents, and so forth? What research and practices are available to me to study?"

The ACTS Model

In answering these questions, I discovered the model I personally was applying in my classroom. I will share my journey of discovery as an example for your own. Because education so desperately needs more acronyms, I'll call my model ACTS, for Applied Curriculum Teaching Strategies (see Figure 4.1).

In all my years of dance, piano, voice, and drama training, I took few written tests. My teachers rarely lectured but gave immediate (and occasionally brutal) feedback. My teachers never assumed my level of learning based on my age, nor did they place me in a class or group by my birth date or the first letter of my last name. Often they gave me individualized practice or exercise routines.

I absolutely loved nearly every course and teacher and the learning stayed with me and transferred to every area of my life. I can still remember music I memorized more than 30 years ago, and "The show must go on" became a philosophy of life. What did I do in these lessons that had such deep effect? I spent nearly all of my time doing one of three things: exercising, practicing, or performing.

In analyzing how these three activities (which apply equally to athletics) affect learning, this is what I realized:

- Exercise internalizes content or concept or skill.
- Practice transfers it.
- Performance applies and spirals back to practice and exercise.

These components are not sequential, but cyclical, interwoven, and interdependent. If one component is missing, the learning experience is incomplete.

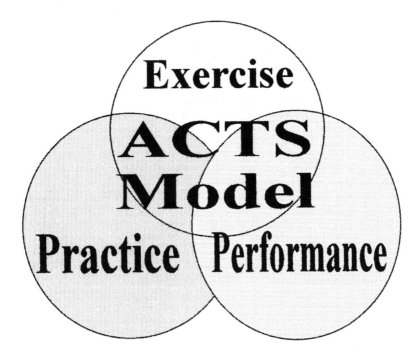

Teaching in the performing arts and athletics is based on three separate but interdependent activities, creating an applied curriculum, one in which skills are modeled and practiced, independently drilled, and put into practice in real situations.

Figure 4.1. The Applied Curriculum Teaching Strategies (ACTS) Model.

EXERCISE

Exercise is the independent drill component. It is the least fun, but it is nonetheless indispensable. Although often considered deadly and boring, repetitive exercise nevertheless remains the only way human fingers can master the violin or piano, human muscle can stretch and tone, and human gray cells can store mathematical facts.

We can create games and goals, make it a whole-group or team activity, all of which work and help. But ultimately, the learner bears responsibility for this "skill-and-drill" component. One reason is the only person who can master scales and arpeggios or the free throw, the only one who can put $6 \times 4 = 24$ into long-term memory, is the learner.

Another reason is that exercise is very individualized. We need drill for what we personally cannot do; we need simple "flexing" exercise to maintain what we can do—one reason why whole-class drills can be more painful than productive. In my performing arts lessons, it was considered "messing around" or wasting time if I spent exercise time going over what I already knew how to do. The point was to work on what I still couldn't do. Learner motivation to exercise comes from the component most often missing in public schools: performance.

PERFORMANCE

We sweat and exercise for the *performance payoff*. Few of us will exercise consistently without this. As research maintains that learning is naturally cyclical, not linear, exercise cycles to performance, which in turn shows us where we need more exercise. We rehearse our lines at night, alone in our rooms, so we can be in the play. We play scales so we can be in the marching band. We do push-ups and run around the field so we can play in the homecoming game. Exercise provides the basic skills. Performance provides the real-world, personally relevant, and motivating application.

Computer scientist Alan Kay (1995) writes:

> One of the great problems with the way most schools are set up is that the children quickly sense that most of the stuff they are asked to do is not "real," especially as opposed to optional activities like sports and games, art and music. They "know" these are "real," and a school has to go to great lengths to make them artificial enough for the children to lose interest. (p. 5)

Leslie Hart (1983) writes in terms of the importance of input in human brain-compatible learning:

> What may be called the reality principle . . . seems to be a neglected but critically important aspect of input. Shooting at a basketball hoop offers a sharp example. One shoots; the ball either goes in or it does not. If it misses, the shooter does not need anyone . . . to say whether or not the shot was successful. That

information which we can loosely call feedback, comes directly and usually instantly from the reality. . . .

In a teaching situation, . . . the student must wait for the teacher . . . to evaluate and provide verbal feedback. A letter to the mayor (not to be sent) is written as an exercise; it is not a real letter, a communication intended to produce some outcome. (p. 73)

Performances are real, and it is this element that produces their "payoff" for the learner. It is impossible to describe the excitement, the self-confidence that comes from performing, except to an athlete, an entertainer, or a student who has just developed a product and sold it to the public or designed a structure, built it, and watched others use it. Unlike a school test, the arts or athletic performance or school project lifts the learner beyond previous levels, even in defeat. She or he goes back to rehearsal and even exercise with renewed commitment.

PRACTICE

The other ACTS component is practice or rehearsal, usually done with others, often in small groups as well as with the whole group. Artists of all kinds do rehearsals or run-throughs. Athletes play intramural games or have practice matches. Practice usually consists of "chunking," that is, dividing performance requirements into manageable segments and working repeatedly on each, then regrouping in different segments to bridge the gaps created by previous segments and see where the weak spots remain, and finally, reuniting segments as a whole.

Note that such division is not usually sequential or incremental, but skill based or people based. For example, baseball practice doesn't consist of working on the beginning, middle, and end of a game, but on throwing, batting, catching, running, and so on. Actors don't continually rehearse the beginning, middle, and end of a play, or the easier, more difficult, and then harder scenes; rehearsals may be scheduled by who is in the scene, or where it takes place.

For practice to be effective, it is crucial to mimic a real situation at some point—to go from beginning to end without stopping to make corrections. Problems stand out in bold relief in such a practice, pointing out where further exercise and sectional drilling are needed.

In school, cooperative groups work on tasks together. Often, however, the task is completed ("Who got the right answer?") rather than analyzed for strengths and for weaknesses needing more exercise, then repeated to measure improvement. Nevertheless, practice seems the component most well addressed in school.

Projects: Framework for the ACTS Model

"Meaningful projects taking place over time and involving various forms of individual and group activity are the most promising vehicles for learning," according to Howard Gardner (1991, p. 204). When I read this, I couldn't help hearing Mickey Rooney say to Judy Garland, "Let's put on a show!"

Projects are different from units or themes. In the words of Morgan (1983),

> project-based learning . . . [is] an activity in which students develop an understanding of a topic or issue through some kind of involvement in an actual . . . real-life problem . . . and in which they have some degree of responsibility in designing their learning activities. (p. 66)

In other words, projects are performances for which multiple rehearsals and extended practice are required. There are basically two types of classroom projects: culminating and ongoing.

CULMINATING PROJECTS

Culminating projects end, after 1 to 8 weeks, in some type of special culminating performance activity. They are most like a play or a show. They involve lots of different types of activities, skills, and groups in their preparation, as well as a good deal of individual or self-directed work.

Using a play as an academic example, students may write everything from advertising copy and programs to the play itself. They may measure classmates for costumes, stage areas for sets, gallons of paint, running time, and rehearsal time. They may count lines and props or calculate costs and profits at various ticket prices. They may calendar performance date(s) and preceding deadlines for finishing sets and costumes, printing posters and programs, knowing lines, and so forth.

In my classes, students not only put on plays but made items to sell, planned class parties, and organized car washes with the same gusto and academic applications. Once I analyzed the model I was using for these activities, I could more carefully balance basic skills exercises with cooperative learning practice, thus strengthening not only learning but the performance payoff and its resulting motivation for further learning.

ONGOING PROJECTS

Other types of projects are ongoing, like a monthly newspaper, a garden, or a recycling service. There are a couple of reasons why I found this type of project seems to take a little more experience on the part of both teacher and students. One reason is that it typically seems harder to consistently involve the whole class.

For example, a newspaper involves computer time to configure final copy and pictures, add headlines, amd so on. Even if each student has a networked computer, there comes a time when decisions must be made by one or two editors alone. A garden may not accommodate your entire class all at one time. And you may not want your whole class picking up recycling from other classrooms at the same time.

Another reason is that the performance payoff comes not in one big event, but gradually over time. Students must be more self-directed, able to work on tasks during study times, or to otherwise occupy themselves if they finish early during project time. They also must have learned to delay gratification, another trait involving acquired self-discipline and some prior experience that has shown them what they're getting is worth waiting for. Finally, there is a curve of parent and site support: high at the beginning, low as the novelty wears off, and gradually rebuilding as ongoing results establish pride and commitment.

Ongoing projects are incredible learning tools. A great many teachers use them, with tremendous success. Completing a couple of culminating projects first seems to build the community pride, self-discipline, self-direction, and teamwork that make ongoing projects more successful.

NARRATIVE OF A CULMINATING PROJECT

I like students to make their own class money and keep track of it in a checking account, for the math, organizational, and life skills involved. After preassessing all my second graders during September on money, time, measurement, addition and subtraction facts, and writing, I asked the kids if they would like to make holiday cards to raise money, which they could then spend on a Halloween party. I was fully prepared with a couple of other ideas in case they were negative or lukewarm about the cards, but they really liked the idea, and so we were off and running.

How much would we sell the cards for? I introduced the concept of packaging and gave a teacher imperative (because I wanted to reinforce counting by 10s and addition and subtraction to 10, and to begin decimals): There would be 10 cards in each pack. If we sold each pack for $1, how much were we charging for each card? How about at $1.50 per pack? We stopped planning for several minutes to work kinesthetically with decimals (passing a basketball left and right along a row of students holding numbers). Then we reviewed prices per pack and prices per card before going on to discuss the party.

How much money did we need for our Halloween party? We began brainstorming about what we would have at the party: food, games, decorations. The class divided into teams. Each team discussed how much money they thought they'd need, while I went from group to group getting a sense of who had a concept of money and price and who did not.

When the teams had individually agreed on what they'd need, we worked as a class on what everything would cost. We wrote, discussed, and totaled all the committee estimates, then added a few dollars for "just in case," coming up with a budget of $25 for our party. With 28 students, we quickly saw that if each person sold a pack of cards for $1, we'd have more than enough money for our party. The idea of having money left over was very exciting to the students. I took the opportunity to mention that we'd just multiplied 28 by 1 (and divided 28 by 25) to get our answer. We multiplied some other things by 1.

Then we took out our calendars. We planned the date for the party, which happened to fall on the 29th. We discussed when the decorations would have to be put up (the morning of the 29th), when they'd have to be completed (the 28th), how long they'd take to make (one week), and when they'd have to be started (the 21st). We did the same with the food and games committees.

The 21st seemed to be our earliest deadline for needing money. That meant we'd have to have all the cards sold by then. We discussed how long it would take to sell them and decided on one week. That meant all cards had to be done by the 14th, which gave us exactly 2 weeks to make them. We saw that school weeks have 5 days, not 7. Two weeks times 5 days = 10 days for 10 cards = one card per day in order to be done on time. We talked about the math that we had done to get our answer and I introduced the term *division*.

Finally, we spent 15 minutes or so drafting possible designs and greetings on recycled paper, and a group volunteered to create a class logo for our packaging. We'd spent nearly an hour and a half on our first project doing whole-group and small-group practice, mostly in the area of math, and the kids didn't want to stop.

The next day we voted on logo designs for our packaging and began working on cards. Each day we worked at least half an hour, during which I was busy facilitating: getting supplies and helping with spelling, punctuation, designs, and packaging. Students were counting and using ordinal numbers and estimating and projecting without my asking them to. "I've got six more done, so I only have four more to do and I'll have another pack—my third!—and that's $3." Some kids made cards for all occasions; others made all-of-a-kind packs. Our practice activities now extended from math to language arts, visual arts, and some social studies (multicultural holidays and customs).

A week prior to our first scheduled selling day I asked how many people felt expert in counting money. "Oh." They'd been too busy to think of that. Some of them knew how. "Will you be able to make change?" I asked. "Oh." "Oh, dear," I worried aloud, "How are you going to learn to count money and make change in just 4 more days?"

They wanted to sell those cards. The room buzzed. Math books appeared from the depths of desks and backpacks. I was informed of a money lesson on pages 166 and 167—the student brought the book to show me. I thanked him and wrote the page numbers on the board.

Within 10 minutes there were page numbers all over the board and students were furiously copying them at their desks. "If you want to take these home and do them as homework, I'll correct them for you and help you with what you don't understand," I offered. They all decided to do at least two pages by the next day. One girl did 16. I love intrinsic motivation!

I designed a receipt that asked customers to pay in coin, not paper, forcing the children to count the money and record it. After selling all the cards, we put all the money on a big table and re-counted it, rolling the coins. We opened a bank account and everyone got a copy of the check register, which we used throughout the year to record our deposits and withdrawals. Our Halloween party was a roaring success and we had $37 left in the bank. I also had my first lesson in how to use a performance payoff to stimulate interdisciplinary in-class practice and independent exercise.

EXAMPLE OF AN ONGOING PROJECT

A class store is a fun and challenging ongoing project. The first consideration, in school as in retail, is location, and my 3-4 class this year is using a cart that can be moved out onto campus for selling and then back to the classroom for practice and preparation. Optimal location varies with grade level and site. A portion of the classroom works when space is available. A separate room and display case is nice when groups can work outside the classroom. Special seasons, events, and sales serve as culminating portions within an ongoing project. Getting ready for these usually involves the whole class, whereas ongoing operations may involve only one or two groups at a time.

We started out with a theme-cycle approach:

1. What do we already know (about stores)?
2. What do we want and need to know?
3. How are we going to find out?

Students were surprised and pleased by how much they already knew, while I got a classwide preassessment of our baseline knowledge. Holes in the students' knowledge (like how to figure out profit) were easy to see. Students came up with a variety of people and places where they could learn more about stores, from their parents to the Internet, from the principal to local store owners. In its very first week, our store stimulated independent math and writing exercise and group practice by conducting a customer survey as to pricing and value-added items such as school emblems.

Currently, my 3-4 class is preparing for a back-to-school sale of donated notebooks. Teams are setting up an inventory system (inventory-purchasing team), decorating our sales cart (display team), preparing school posters and taped commercials (publicity team), practicing making change and serving customers (sales team), and coordinating our business hours with the student council and the office (management team). Meanwhile, I am conducting individual baseline assessments in reading and math.

Before our initial sale is over, the purchasing and publicity groups will begin preparing for Halloween. The display, sales, and management committees will follow, while the purchasing and publicity groups move on to work the winter holiday season. The management team serves a crucial function in keeping information flowing among the teams, helping coordinate their efforts with each other and with the rest of the school, and overseeing the calendaring of work and events.

All the teams are interdependent. Display must coordinate closely with both purchasing and publicity, publicity with display and sales, and sales with publicity and purchasing. Actually feeling this interdependence takes some time for the students, but it is a powerful part of the performance payoff and an excellent lesson in necessary life skills. Each team stresses slightly different skills. Purchasing is more mathematical-logical; display more visual-spatial and kinesthetic; publicity more verbal and musical; and sales more interpersonal, verbal, and mathematical. Management requires a bit of all seven (or more) areas of intelligence, including intrapersonal. In January, after another series of assessments, students will have the opportunity to work on new teams.

PROJECT TIPS

Daily progress check-ins with team leaders are important, as are periodic whole-class updates during the hour or so per day spent on project work. And, as with any group work, it's important to monitor individuals who are leaving all the work to someone else or who are being excluded by their peers. This is particularly true in middle school, where students have acquired solid reputations for not contributing in group work, reputations that must be reversed for the process to work. Fortunately, the built-in motivation provided by the performance aspect can go a long way toward reworking reputations for the better. Natural consequences are important, too. For example, if your refreshments team forgets to bring drinks the day of the party, have the party without the drinks, because the planning lesson is more important than the beverages.

At first, students many not know what to do; responsibility and self-direction take some getting used to (for all of us). It often takes one complete project for some students to feel comfortable, and they will more fully participate in the second. However, culminating projects can and do go well on the first try and in a short time. At a year-round middle school where students were referred to intersession (summer school) for low grades or poor behavior, classroom teachers watching our final performance were surprised by the level of engagement from their students. Due to the pride and ownership that develops during projects, initial results may seem far more impressive to the students (of all ages) than to the teacher.

Additional project examples and ideas from teachers across the country can be acquired through an Educational Resources Information Center (ERIC) computer search, particularly for middle and secondary students. Those not yet on-line may dial 1-800 LET ERIC for assistance.

Performance Assessments: Testing the ACTS Model

For projects to work in an academic setting, baseline (pre-) assessments and ongoing and culminating (post-) assessments are vital. Beginning projects with a theme cycle (What do you already know?) and culminating them with products or performances makes assessment somewhat built in, but postassessments must still be recorded next to corresponding preassessments and change noted. Two math performance assessment examples (Figures 4.2a, 4.2b. 4.3a, and 4.3b) follow that may be given in stations operated by older students, advanced peers, or adult volunteers. These operate like miniperformances, making areas for growth (practice and exercise) readily apparent to both teacher and student (and parent, when kept in the portfolio), all in an enjoyable and stress-free atmosphere.

The station leader asks specific questions (like those accompanying each assessment) so that each student will have the same test as every other student and pre- and posttesting will be consistent.

No coaching is allowed. Students respond using actual (or at least hands-on) materials. Their responses are recorded as simply and nonjudgmentally as possible: a check if they were right, an "X" if wrong, or their actual numerical answer. No "That's right!" or "Oops!" responses from station leaders.

Students should carry a book or sketchpad with them in case they have to wait at a station. There should be two or three separate sets of materials and more than one leader at stations that take a good deal of time. It's good to print the assessment sheet on heavy-weight paper like construction paper, both for durability and for easy access in the student's portfolio. Using a different color paper for pre- and postassessments is helpful.

The information supplied by performance assessments is free of the reading and writing biases of old test forms. Including several skills on one sheet shows at a glance how students may be grouped for practice, who peer coaches or "class experts" might be in the various areas, and areas where the entire class needs practice.

Students enjoy these assessments, seeing them as stress-free, more like games. Because they are demonstrating skills rather than supplying answers, they do not mind repeating the same assessments before and after a project or periodically. Also, they can see—without humiliation—the areas in which they need exercise and practice.

A model like ACTS gives the teacher two sets of instructional guidelines: a natural, personal, cyclical curriculum base and exercise, practice, performance activities. Once we have such a model, we can examine our curriculum, our teaching style, and the details of our days and ask questions like these:

1. Whose learning theory or what research is it based on?
2. Is it personally relevant to learners, natural (brain based), and cyclical?
3. Is it exercise, practice, or performance based?
4. What is the expected outcome?
5. How is it being pre- and postassessed?

The ACTS model and the projects and assessments that complement it all came from my personal areas of interest and expertise.

(text continues on page 70)

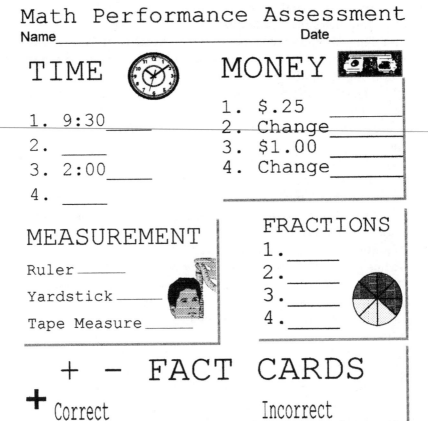

Math Performance Assessment

Name_____   Date_____

TIME

1. 9:30_____
2. _____
3. 2:00_____
4. _____

MONEY

1. $.25 _____
2. Change_____
3. $1.00 _____
4. Change_____

MEASUREMENT

Ruler_____
Yardstick_____
Tape Measure_____

FRACTIONS

1. _____
2. _____
3. _____
4. _____

+ - FACT CARDS

+ Correct _____   Incorrect _____

- Correct _____   Incorrect _____

Figure 4.2a. Math Performance Assessment, Part I

Math Performance Assessment Directions

Station leader's questions are in regular type. *Directions for recording answers are in italics.* Needed: a large clock face with movable hands for the student to manipulate, real money, measuring tools, 3 unifix cubes, and addition and subtraction flash card sets.

TIME

1. Show 9:30 on the clock. *(Record the actual time shown by the student.)*
2. What time is it? *(Set the clock for 6:00 and record what the student says.)*
3. Show 2:00 on the clock. *(Record the time set by the student.)*
4. What time is it? *(Set 12:30 and record the student's answer.)*

MONEY

1. Show me 25 cents. *(Check if the student gets it right; cross out if wrong.)*
2. How much is this? *(Show the student 15 cents. Record his or her answer.)*
3. Show me one dollar. *(Check if right; cross out if wrong.)*
4. What's this? *(Show 60 cents. Record the answer given.)*

MEASUREMENT

(Give the student a ruler, a yardstick and a measuring tape. Ask him or her to measure the desk or table you are using and put the answer on the back of the assessment sheet with words, numbers, and/or pictures. Put a check by the measuring tool(s) the student uses.)

FRACTIONS

1. *(Show the student three unifix cubes joined together.)* If this is a whole, show me 1/3. *(Check if OK; cross out if wrong.)*
2. Show me 2/3. *(Check if OK; cross out if wrong.)*
3. Show me 1/2. *(Write what the student says/does— "can't," "1/3," etc.)*
4. *(Separate the unifix cubes.)* Show me a whole. *(Check if OK; cross out if wrong.)*

FLASH CARDS

1. *(Show 25 addition flash cards for about 3 seconds each. Place correct responses in one pile, incorrect responses in another. Record the number right and wrong.)*
2. *(Repeat Step 1 for subtraction flash cards.)*

Figure 4.2b. Math Performance Assessment, Part II

Figure 4.3a. Performance Assessment, Part I

Performance Assessment Directions

Since this particular assessment requires no props or setup, one station leader can give the entire assessment to each of five or six students. Students do not have to move from station to station but may stay in table groups or work on other activities while waiting for their turn. Spoken directions to the student are in regular type. *Station leader directions are in italics.*

CALENDAR

(Record the student's answers in the four blank boxes at the end of the month.)
1. How many days are in October?
2. Show me a week. *(Check if OK; cross out if incorrect.)*
3. How many days are in a week? 2 weeks? *(Use a slash [/] between answers.)*
4. If today is the 8th, what day of the week is it?

CLOCKS

(Record answers in blanks by clocks.)
1. What time is it on the top clock?
2. What time is it on the bottom clock?

SHOPPING LIST

Write a shopping list for the grocery store.

BUILDINGS

Estimate (don't count) how many buildings.

SORTING

Decide whether each object in the box belongs with Object #1 or with Object #2 at the left. Write 1 or 2 under each object in the box.

Bonus: How much money is in the box? Put your answer in the blank next to the dollar sign on top of the box.

Figure 4.3b. Performance Assessment, Part II

Drawing on personal background, analyzing how learning was organized there, applying learning theory and research to determine why learning was occurring, and synthesizing everything into an academic classroom approach was an exciting process of growth and personal power for me as a teacher. Like every other model, ACTS will not work for every teacher or student. But it is grounded in centuries of successful practice; prima ballerinas, opera stars, and Olympic athletes have succeeded with it. It is supported by educational theory and research and is personal, natural, and cyclical. It is in line with new-paradigm thinking, empowering the teacher as well as the students. Many other models will meet all these criteria, too. It is up to each of us to find the one that is most comfortable and appropriate.

Defining Our Information-Age Teaching Style

As we saw in Chapter 3, in redefining our role in teaching, we are automatically redefining our students' role, too. As our personal power increases, so must theirs. For many of our students, the increase in responsibility for their own learning will come as a bit of a shock, accustomed as they are to the recipient culture of television, where all they have to do is show up. For some teachers, too, the ability to pursue their own ideas rather than rigidly adhere to someone else's may seem foreign at first. Still, freedom and individuality are heady possessions and, once appreciated, not lightly forfeited.

When we try to impose teaching styles from the top down, we keep teachers dependent and incapable, that is, unable to function without direction and supervision. They then, in turn, must produce dependent and incapable students. This was fine when that was the type of graduate that business wanted—someone to do boring, repetitive tasks; someone to take orders without asking questions; someone to let the bosses do the thinking. Now, we say we want students who think, who are self-directed, independent, lifelong learners. But we cannot produce this kind of person out of our current system. Freedom is not about control; it's about letting go.

An Information-Age network system will operate differently from a hierarchy, and the changes we make to help bring this about will affect not only how we feel about ourselves but also what we do in our work. Applying brain research and the new science, we now know that actual experiences engage more of the brain than reading or listening, that input foreign to our daily experience is more difficult to enter into long-term memory. We now believe that there are many forms of intelligence, not just those measured by language and mathematics. We know that the whole is greater than the sum of its parts, that breaking things down into steps may destroy useful information rather than increase it, and that focusing on content without context can destroy meaning.

We now know that "Attention drives learning and memory. . . . Our attentional system determines what is important, and you never remember anything if it's not important" (Sylwester, 1995, p. 4). Because television has shortened attention spans, we can turn to models like ACTS because the performing arts and athletics have always increased attention span and the ability to focus.

As we work toward a more independent role for ourselves, we can help our students to become more independent and self-directed. This reinforces our role as the facilitator, or so-called "guide-on-the-side," as opposed to the source of all information (now impossible) or "sage-on-the-stage."

Traditional Styles: Direct and Indirect Teaching

To be sure, some students will always prefer or need a more traditional style. But it's definitely true that their numbers are declining, due to change in the surrounding culture. All of us have been taught in the style called direct teaching or teacher directed, a hierarchical style where the teacher tells the students what and how they will learn and be tested, and the students (clearly in a "lesser" position) follow the prescribed routine.

Indirect teaching actually follows much the same format but is couched in student-oriented language. Students, often in groups, make learning choices from within a limited selection. Both styles lend themselves to a prescribed, one-size-fits-all curriculum and an incremental (step-by-step, linear) approach. Both are obviously in line with the old paradigm and just as obviously what both teachers and the general public think of as school.

Self-Directed Learning

This style focuses on the learner, not the teacher. In it, the teacher facilitates by setting up situations rich in concepts to be discovered and skills to be exercised and practiced. Individual learners choose areas of focus and participation and work to exceed their prior individual levels. This style is based on firsthand experience and begins by assessing learners' prior knowledge and interests. It embodies transfer and application of skills and concepts into different modalities (for example, spatial, musical, and kinesthetic) as part of its application, performance, and assessment phase.

Dr. Guy Duckworth, while at Northwestern University in the 1960s, taught a vivid description of the three styles, the gist of which is, I hope, recaptured here:

> Suppose you wanted students to understand the concept of a chain reaction, so you set up a box of dominoes in an "S" pattern on a table before class. In the direct method, you would tell the class that you were going to show them a chain reaction, asking them to carefully watch what happened when you tipped over the first domino. After letting them watch the dominoes collapse in sequence, you might ask students to re-create the event, or to write about what they observed.
>
> In the indirect method, you might ask one of the students to come up front to the table and tip over the first domino while the rest of the class observed the result. Or you might have set up centers where you'd ask groups to choose one person to tip over the first domino, discuss the result, and report back to the class.
>
> In the learner-directed method, you would tell students they had a certain amount of time to examine the domino sets. If no one ventured to touch the first domino, you could stop, coming back to the task later until someone discovered the principle of chain reactions. The power of this last method is that the learning belongs to the students, as in the Chinese proverb: "I hear and I forget. I see and I remember. I do and I understand."

* * *

Whenever other teachers and I discuss major changes in public teaching, the question "How would you change the system to do that?" inevitably arises. To answer the question fully is the subject of another book. There is ample evidence in the study of natural systems (Capra, 1983, 1991, 1996), in the trends foreseen for future organizations (Naisbitt, 1994, Toffler & Toffler, 1995), in the new configurations of business (Pinchot & Pinchot, 1994), and in the emerging world of the Internet (Gates, 1995) that the new system we create will likely be an international network of interrelated and interconnected, yet independent, local minisystems—simultaneously and paradoxically (Naisbitt, 1994) more connected at the national and global levels and more locally autonomous.

However, the point is not what *my* answer would be nor even what the experts predict, but what *our* answers—both individually and collectively—*will be*. If we are to truly redefine the tools, conditions, status, and responsibilities of teaching, we cannot allow someone else to "give us" a new system. We must be an integral part of its design, one that supports—not inhibits—the ways we believe we should teach.

There are more sources for ideas than we may realize. Just as the ACTS curricular model comes from the performing arts and athletics, so does an entire education system, a network of private studios and gyms reaching around the globe, founded on traditions hundreds of years old, yet often incorporating the most current research and methods. There are the private worldwide academic systems, like Waldorf and Montessori, and there are the public systems in other countries. Our task is to open ourselves to the new worldview and then to remain open to any and all educational possibilities that might fit it.

Surely we are as creative as those minds who conjured up our current system. Certainly we have access to more information about learning than they did. By raising our awareness and self-confidence to higher levels, we can begin to see beyond what is and to envision and create what could be.

5

Embracing the New View

Procrustes was a mean old man whose acquaintance one makes when studying Latin or Greek mythology. His enormous house stood by a lonely road in the mythical Attican countryside. Travelers caught by nightfall and seeking shelter found that Procrustes had but one guest bed, and one grave idiosyncrasy: his guests must fit that bed. Thus he measured everyone, tying all to the iron bedstead and stretching those too short, dismembering those too tall. Theseus slew Procrustes, but his spirit lives on in public education.

BLACK, IN BLACK, CAMPBELL, AND BRIDGES, 1992, P. 1

What We're Up Against

Along myriad complex paths paved with good intentions and as many false assumptions—not to mention a little panic—education has arrived at the edge of a precipice. We are aware that our next steps are crucial.

We are aware that this year's reforms can supplant last year's before those are fully functional. Programs implemented simultaneously can actually contradict each other. Rushing to get programs in place for "this year's graduates" can yield years stuck with rush-job versions. Teachers who work hard to contribute to programs or innovations may find their work cut short or stretched out of shape as other programs usurp time, staff, space, or funding. And even very successful programs and teacher contributions may tend, over time, to lose impact. All these factors prove disheartening to teachers who give extra time and effort only to see the return on that effort fade.

> I know there must be schools you think are exceptions. . . . [T]rouble is that when fundamental rights depend on some-one's whim you really have no rights, only privileges which may be withdrawn at any minute. . . . Special teachers in this sort of experiment last until the key administrator retires. (Gatto, 1995, p. 7)

Regardless of the quality of reforms, regardless of the perform-ance of individual districts or sites under specific leadership, the Procrustean system in which all these efforts exist will gradually chop off a piece here, stretch a program there, as it works back to-ward its steady state: uniformity. And the system is totally right in doing so, because that's exactly what a good Industrial-Age bureau-cracy was designed to do. The problem is that the world is now in the Information Age. It's time education was, too.

Why We Can't Wait

"Teachers cannot afford to wait for the system to change itself. They must push for the kind of professional culture they want, sometimes in the face of unresponsive principals, communities and school districts" (Fullan, 1993, p. 81). Our new worldview comes in a flash. "The new paradigm is not 'figured out' but suddenly seen" (Ferguson, 1980, p. 27). Once we "get it," it seems obvious and affects everything we do. Until then, we talk about reforms and new pro-grams and targets and goals and issues, as though the system we are working in still made sense.

It doesn't. And the time for talk may be shorter than we think. Our world has already been forever altered by a new view of reality; meanwhile our old worldview has brought us to a point in time that environmentalists feel is pivotal to our survival (Athanasiou, 1996). "Over 1,670 scientists, including 104 Nobel laureates" have signed the 1992 document, The World's Scientists' Warning to Humanity, which states that "human beings and the natural world are on a col-lision course. . . . If not checked, many of our current practices . . .

may so alter the living world that it will be unable to sustain life in the manner that we know" (Ehrlich & Ehrlich, 1996, p. 246).

Education has an important role to play as our very culture redefines itself, and we, as teachers, are vital to that role. Rather than debating which math or reading curriculum to adopt districtwide, we need to widen our focus to participate in the much larger questions facing our profession and our culture.

> Cultures get changed in a thousand small ways, not by dramatic announcements from the boardroom. If we wait until top management gives leadership to the change we want to see, we miss the point. For us to have any hope that our own preferred future will come to pass, we provide the leadership. (Block, as quoted in Fullan, 1993, p. 14)

It is time for teachers to become independent, informed, entrepreneurial thinkers. It is time for us to take charge of our work, take on the responsibilities and rewards of professionals, and connect with others in our profession in a constant cycle of growth, improvement, and learning. It is time for the heightened awareness, the liberation, the suffrage of the teacher. It's time for a New Teacher.

Because "when placed in the same systems, people, however different tend to produce similar results" (Senge, 1990, p. 42), the role of a New Teacher is not only to teach but to define a new education system—or systems. If we can find the wisdom to stop fiddling while Rome burns and the courage to face real issues like the sustainability of life on our planet, the educational task before us will pale into its proper perspective. We can stop clinging to the old and start creating the new.

What We Can Do

This book is not intended to tell teachers *what* to think or *how* to act but simply to think and to act in ways based on where we are going, not where we've been. If we would redefine teaching, if we would claim our new voice, we must be informed—about the world, and about other ways of seeing and living in it. We must take part in local and global change and dispel the myth that "Those who can't do, teach."

We must learn about the new forms organizations are taking, about the latest research into learning and the brain, and about the differences between what constitutes knowledge in the past and knowledge in the present and future. We must learn about sustainability. We must learn all we can about technology and how it is already changing the way people learn, how it could shape teaching in completely new ways (see Davis & Botkin, 1994), and how we can use it to greater advantage personally.

We must make other teachers aware of what we're learning; we must educate them and parents and the general public. Fortunately, that's exactly what we're good at. We must encourage the intelligence, creativity, industry, judgment, and valor of the best and brightest minds we can bring to teaching in order to give us the means to educate our culture—the lever Archimedes sought with which to move the world.

We also must quit accepting the blame for our culture's ills and start directing the changes that could cure them. Part of claiming our voice is letting people know what's really going on in schools today and what we think could be done about it. If people don't realize where or what the problem actually is, they'll go right on trying to rearrange the deck chairs on the Titanic so they don't slope so much.

While we work for personal and systemic change, we need to act with assertiveness when new programs, procedures, and training are required of us; that is, we need to request the reasoning, theories, and research on which they were selected and ask for additional planning time and materials, funds for implementation, a set incubation period, and the name of the current program(s) they are *replacing*. These requests are reasonable and professional; they seem fantastic only in light of our usual frenetic and dysfunctional working conditions.

We must ask that personally relevant coursework count for staff development. We must fully utilize the talents and training teachers already have. We must ask intelligent questions that require intelligent answers. We must form and join networks and support groups. In addition, we must work always for more choice for ourselves and our students.

One caution: it is vital that we recognize that radically new or different ideas may draw criticism as much from others' fear as from any inadequacy of the idea itself. Those who have devoted their lives to public education have no other frame of reference. Threats to this frame feel personal.

Recently, I attended a weekend teacher training put on by a highly reputable private nonprofit group. During one of the activities, a small team of us discussed the developmental grouping used in a particular private school, and Dorothy (name changed) and I continued this discussion during break.

Dorothy asserted that because the school in question was private, its practices held no value for public education, that what works in private programs simply cannot be applied to public schools because they operate under different rules: Private schools can choose their students. I suggested that this stance potentially precluded some good ideas and techniques from being tried in public schools. She maintained, "If the sample's tainted, it's tainted. Period." Why, then, had she flown across country and paid for 2 nights' lodging to attend workshops conducted by a private institution (with attendance by invitation only) if nothing she learned there would apply to her public school classroom?

We must be prepared to understand that this kind of argument does not mean the person's reasoning is faulty, but that fear may have *eclipsed* their reasoning. They may hope that everything is "really okay" and is going to remain basically the same. It's a comforting thought. Similarly, we'd all like to think that we can just close our doors and teach and it will all go away. But it's too late: We know better.

Tribute Due the Current System

Before closing, it's important to acknowledge that the current system of education, although now outdated, is certainly not without merit, that much good has come of it, and that many very devoted people have lived lives of service within its frame. We have the most highly and widely educated populace in history because of it. You and I can communicate through the symbols on this paper because of it. We must recognize that it will not be an easy thing for any of us to let it go. Nothing in these pages is meant to contradict any of this.

Bridges (1991) reminds us, "When endings take place, people get angry, sad, frightened, depressed, confused . . . the natural sequence of emotions people go through when they lose something that matters to them" (p. 24) and "People have to reorient themselves psychologically if the situational difference is going to work" (p. 4). Leaving behind the old system will represent a loss, and we must be prepared to feel the loss without feeling that something is wrong with us or with what we are trying to do.

We're leaving the familiar behind. We've all been there. Although some of us loved it and some of us didn't, the experience of school has changed little in more than 100 years (Hart, 1983, p. 12), leaving us as teachers to expect what we experienced as students, and putting parents, business, and the rest of society in the same position. These old expectations, held in common, can make true change more difficult to imagine, the old structure so taken for granted that it becomes invisible. (It's hard to see the forest when you're standing in the middle of all those trees.) We may fear entering a time of the unexpected and unfamiliar.

For those, like Dorothy above, who have not yet accepted that change of the magnitude herein discussed is both inevitable and essential, fear can manifest as denial that anything needs radical changing in the first place or that change of great scope is possible. But as in grief, denial is the first step in the change process. We must respect our own and others' transitionary states, lend support and encouragement whenever we can, ask for support and encouragement when we need it, and remember that transitions are—thankfully—temporary.

> Yes, fears must be respected and learned about, but they must not paralyze us, or lure us into a half-life of being afraid all the time. I like to think of my fears being driven away in a Rolls Royce. (For it is true that once you face a fear, it loses all of its stuffing, and will sit quietly in the back seat and do as it's told. (SARK, 1992, p. 71)

What We Can Expect

We can expect hard work and a sometimes uphill battle, but we have those now. We can also expect more self-respect, more personal power and freedom, more sense of accomplishment, and a new professionalism, because those will come.

The 10% that is choosing that path for the sake of health and wholeness has more power ultimately than the 90% that is fighting to remain where it is and have its own way, because the Universe backs that 10% and not the 90%. (Zukav, 1989, p. 142)

We are on the path of becoming New Teachers, improving and growing each day, looking ahead at our careers, regardless of years already served. Our "newness" is our attitude, not our time slot. Our strength lies in our alignment with our times, in the connections we will make with each other, and in the completeness we seek within ourselves.

The strongest message a teacher can deliver to children is a statement of his or her own aggressive independence. In this lies the formula for the different breed of schoolteacher we need and for schools we never had. Not people grateful for some administrative liberality or for the hollow promise of decision making, but complete people who map their own course. (Gatto, 1995, p. 13)

Staying Connected

This is but a beginning. I, like you, have to return on Monday morning to the world as it currently is. However, I go as a New Teacher, with my attitude firmly in place.

I will keep a journal of my successes daily and I will communicate them to both parents and staff. If challenged, I will quote chapter and verse of current research and theory, and refer again to my successes.

I will view all mistakes and failures as opportunities for learning, not reasons to hide. I will deal with paperwork and testing as quickly and efficiently as possible, having students help. I will ask students (and parents) to evaluate programs imposed on us.

I will constantly remember that other learning systems already exist "out there": private arts studios and athletics programs, independent academic schools like Waldorf and Montessori, other national and cultural approaches, and technology that is affecting everything. I will draw from their strengths.

I will remember that people often think they like to be given answers. (Chapter 4 is the one fellow teachers liked best, probably because it seems to provide some answers.) I will try, as I do with my students, to challenge people's thinking, not give answers.

And I will remember the story of the "Hundredth Monkey":

> Thus, when a certain critical number achieves an awareness, this new awareness may be communicated from mind to mind. ... There is a point at which if only one more person tunes-in to a new awareness, a field is strengthened so that this awareness reaches almost everyone! (Keyes, Jr., 1983, p. 17)

In truth, any one of us, even feeling isolated and alone, could decide to join a network and so complete the critical mass needed to effect critical cultural change. I will not pass up the opportunity to be that "one more person."

These are my promises to myself, and I hope you will make some similar ones of your own. I also promise to be available to share ideas. Please e-mail me at: TEACHNET@aol.com.

> *I am only one; but still I am one. I cannot do everything, but still I can do something; I will not refuse to do the something I can do.*
>
> HELEN KELLER

Glossary of Learning Theories

Adult: "Adults will commit to learning when the goals and objectives are considered realistic and important to them. . . . Adults will learn, retain, and use what they perceive is relevant to their personal and professional needs. . . . Adult learning is ego-involved. . . . Adults need to see the results of their efforts. . . . Adults are much more concrete in the way they operate than formerly thought. . . . Adults who participate in small groups are more likely to move their learning beyond understanding to application, analysis, synthesis, and evaluation. . . . Adults come to learning with a wide range of previous experiences, knowledge, self-direction, interests, and competencies. . . . Adults want to be the origin of their own learning and will resist learning situations that they believe are an attack on their competence. . . . Because the transfer of learning is not automatic for adults, it must be planned for and facilitated" (Wood & Thompson, 1993, pp. 52-57).

"The ways teachers learn may be more like the ways students learn than we have previously recognized" (Lieberman, 1995, p. 592). "If I am the type of teacher I want [teachers] to become, I can't tell them these things about teaching and learning and knowing, I have to teach them those things" (Wilson, 1992, p. 143).

Brain-based: "Brain research establishes and confirms that multiple complex and concrete experiences are essential for meaningful learning and teaching" (Caine & Caine, 1991, p. 5). "Instruction that recognizes and is compatible with the natural (precivilization) brain functions will go far faster and be vastly more successful—much as it is easier to go with the current of a swift river than against it" (Hart, 1983, p. 51). "The ability to make plans and carry them out is the key aspect of human intelligence. . . . Students, told what to do at every turn, get little chance to use their brains in this basic, human way" (Hart, 1983, p. 49).

Chaos: "Disorder can play a critical role in giving birth to new, higher forms of order. . . . Order and chaos . . . are . . . mirror images, one containing the other, a continual process" (Wheatley, 1992, p. 11). "It seems that the very experiences . . . children seek out are ones we avoid: disequilibrium, novelty, loss of control, surprise" (Wheatley, 1992, p. 75).

"In an open classroom . . . each school year is unique for both the students and the teacher. The first day is not filled with the mastery of routines and the pronouncement of rules. It is not possible to anticipate which rules or routines will emerge. . . . Just as one has to suspend expectations with respect to individual students, so with respect to rules and routines one must suspend one's fear of chaos" (Kohl, 1969, p. 29).

Change: "The imposition of change can lead to low morale, dissatisfaction and reduced commitment" (Sikes, 1992, p. 49). Bridges (1991) describes a three-step process for helping people in an organization deal with radical change. First, recognize and celebrate the *ending* that is occurring. Second, understand and respect the *neutral zone,* the period of confusion between the old and the new. Third is the *new beginning* itself, which is successful only if the other two stages were (pp. 4-6).

Collateral: "Perhaps the greatest of all pedagogical fallacies is the notion that a person learns only the particular thing he is studying at the time. Collateral learning in the way of formation of enduring attitudes, of likes and dislikes, may be and often is much more important than the spelling lesson or lesson in geography or history that is learned. For these attitudes are fundamentally what count in the future. The most important attitude that can be formed is that of desire to go on learning" (Dewey, 1938, p. 48).

Creativity: "is a natural potential. . . . incompatible with external and
    internal rewards or punishments. . . . [c]reativity is a prime
    need of a human being and its denial brings about a pervasive
    state of dissatisfaction and boredom" (Bohm & Peat, 1987, pp.
    230-232).

Discovery: "When we watch a child in an environment that is his
    and that evokes response in him, we see that he works by him-
    self toward his own self-perfection. . . . We have exerted the ef-
    fort to get him the things that he needs. Now we must learn to
    take ourselves in hand and watch from the sidelines, following
    him at a distance, neither tiring him with our intervention nor
    abandoning him" (Montessori, 1956, p. 101).

Experiential: Knowledge must arise from and be applicable to real-
    world experiences. "There is an intimate and necessary rela-
    tion between the processes of actual experience and educa-
    tion" (Dewey, 1938, p. 20). "The 18th-century philosopher Jean
    Jacques Rousseau declared in his classic treatise on education,
    Emile, that the child must learn not through words, but
    through experience; not through books but through 'the book
    of life' " (Armstrong, 1994, p. 49). "Learners are empowered by
    the knowledge that they are learners. They are not empow-
    ered by simply acquiring . . . skills" (Freire, quoted in Cox, 1990,
    p. 78).

Future: "An important question to ask of any proposed educational
    innovation is simply this: Is it intended to make the factory run
    more efficiently, or is it designed, as it should be, to get rid of
    the factory model altogether and replace it with individual-
    ized, customized education?" (Toffler & Toffler, 1995, p. 83).
        "The telecommunications revolution will enlarge the role of
    the individual. . . . in the direction of making the smallest
    player in the global economy more and more powerful" (Nais-
    bitt, 1994, p. 357). "When faced with the problem of ignorance,
    we immediately create more and more information without
    seeming to realize that while it may be valuable, it is no substi-
    tute for knowledge—much less wisdom" (Gore, 1993, p. 201).
    "Knowing the right answers must be replaced with learning

how to learn and how to create new solutions" (Land & Jarman, 1992, p. 121).

Intelligent organization: "The transformation from bureaucracy to organizational intelligence is a move from relationships of dominance and submission . . . to . . . relationships of peers across a network of voluntary cooperation" (Pinchot & Pinchot, 1994, p. Xiv).

Multiple intelligences: "Relatively autonomous human intellectual competences. . . . 'frames of mind'. . . . independent of one another . . . can be fashioned and combined in a multiplicity of adaptive ways by individuals and cultures" (Gardner, 1983, pp. 8-9). "These intelligences are fictions—at most, useful fictions—for discussing processes and abilities that (like all of life) are continuous with one another" (Gardner, 1983, p. 70). Multiple intelligences include, but are not limited to, the following categories: linguistic, musical, logical-mathematical, spatial, bodily-kinesthetic, intrapersonal, interpersonal, and naturalist (Gardner, 1997).

Natural knowledge: "is what results when information, felt meaning, and deep meaning come together. The learner has acquired a felt meaning for the subject or concept or procedure so that the new information and procedures fit together. In addition, there is a sufficient connection with the learner's interests or deep meanings so that the information and procedures are personally relevant" (Caine & Caine, 1991, p. 99).

Personal relevance: "It is not enough that certain materials and methods have proved effective with other individuals at other times. There must be a reason for thinking that they will function in generating an experience that has educative quality with particular individuals at a particular time" (Dewey, 1938, p. 46). "A biological structure stands in active relation to the environment. And this relation is knowledge" (Piaget in Furth, 1970, p. 16). "Though one can compel attention, one cannot compel interest. . . . I cannot compel an interest in the children, when the interest does not originate in them" (Neill, 1960, pp. 162-163).

Prior knowledge: Knowledge and skills already held by learners and upon which they can build new knowledge. "We acquire language by understanding input that contains structures that are just beyond our current level of competence" (McElvain, 1995, p. 49, describing Krashin's theory).

Spiral: "Any subject can be taught effectively in some intellectually honest form to any child at any stage of development" (Bruner, 1960, p. 33). "If earlier learning is to render later learning easier . . . the relations between things encountered earlier and later are made as clear as possible. . . . [t]he basic ideas that lie at the heart of all science and mathematics and the basic themes that give form to life and literature are as simple as they are powerful. To be in command of these basic ideas, to use them effectively, requires a continual deepening of one's understanding of them that comes from learning to use them in progressively more complex forms" (Bruner, 1960, pp. 12-13). "Knowledge, learning, understanding, are not linear. They are not little bits of facts lined up in rows or piled up one on top of another" (Holt, 1964, p. 106).

Tabula rasa: Latin for "erased tablet" or "blank slate," meaning the student is an empty page on which the teacher writes information, a vehicle waiting for gas. The teacher's job is the *direct teacher-centered transmission* of information or content.

Transfer: Transferring learning to different situations strengthens students' grasp of the concepts being learned. "Massive general transfer can be achieved by appropriate learning, even to the degree that learning properly under optimum conditions leads one to 'learn how to learn' " (Bruner, 1960, p. 6).
"As an individual passes from one situation to another, his world, his environment, expands or contracts. He does not find himself living in another world, but in a different part or aspect of one and the same world. What he has learned in the way of knowledge and skill in one situation becomes an instrument of understanding and dealing effectively with the situations which follow" (Dewey, 1938, p. 44). "Transference works two ways. It carries ideas from the familiar to the new situation, and from the new back to the familiar" (Black, 1972, p. 26).

Bibliography

Aburdene, P., & Naisbitt, J. (1992). *Megatrends for women.* New York: Random House.

Aitken, L. L., & Mildon, D. A. (1992). Teacher education and the developing teacher: The role of personal knowledge. In M. Fullan & A. Hargreaves (Eds.), *Teacher development and educational change* (pp. 10-35). Bristol, PA: Falmer.

Armstrong, T. (1994). *Multiple intelligences in the classroom.* Alexandria, VA: Association for Supervision and Curriculum Development.

Athanasiou, T. (1996). *Divided planet: The ecology of rich and poor.* Boston: Little, Brown.

Barrentine, P. (Ed.) (1993). *When the canary stops singing.* San Francisco: Berrett-Koehler.

Black, C. (1995). *Pedagogy of the new teacher.* Unpublished master's thesis, San Jose State University, San Jose, CA.

Black, C. L. (1972). *A study of the elements common to dance, drama, and music as a framework for a combined arts curriculum.* Master's thesis, Northwestern University, Evanston, IL.

Black, C. L., Campbell, S., & Bird, L. B. (Eds.) (1992). *Whole learning: A 21st century education design.* Proposal submitted by the Theseus Design Group to New American Schools Development Corporation (NASDC), Arlington, VA.

Bohm, D., & Peat, F. D. (1987). *Science, order, and creativity.* New York: Bantam.

Bridges, W. (1991). *Managing transitions: Making the most of change.* Reading, MA: Addison-Wesley.

Bruner, J. S. (1960). *The process of education.* New York: Vintage.

Bruner, J. S. (1966). *Toward a theory of instruction.* New York: W. W. Norton.

Caine, R. N., & Caine, G. (1991). *Making connections: Teaching and the human brain.* Alexandria, VA: Association for Supervision and Curriculum Development.

California Department of Education Statistics (1991-1992). *Fact sheet: Handbook of education information* (CDOE Publication No. P91-38 CR088784 8-91 5M). Sacramento, CA: State Board of Education Office.

Canfield, J., & Hansen, M. V. (1995). *A second helping of chicken soup for the soul.* Deerfield Beach, FL: Health Communications.

Capra, F. (1983). *The turning point: Science, society, and the rising culture.* New York: Bantam.

Capra, F. (1991). *The tao of physics.* Boston: Shambhala.

Capra, F. (1995a). *Creating community through ecoliteracy: An ecological model for school innovation and reform* [conference pamphlet]. Alexandria, VA: Association for Supervision and Curriculum Development.

Capra, F. (1995b). *Ecoliteracy: Creating vibrant learning communities.* [Cassette Recording No. 95-2518]. Alexandria, VA: Association for Supervision and Curriculum Development.

Capra, F. (1996). *The web of life: A new scientific understanding of living systems.* New York: Anchor/Doubleday.

Castaneda, C. (1968). *The teachings of don Juan: A Yaqui way of knowledge.* New York: Pocket Books.

Celebrating Excellence, Inc. (1991). *Great quotes from great women.* Lombard, IL: Successories Library.

Chopra, D. (1990). *Quantum healing: Exploring the frontiers of mind/body medicine.* New York: Bantam.

Cleary, B. (1968). *Ramona the pest.* New York: William Morrow.

Cohen, P. (1995). Understanding the brain: educators seek to apply brain research. *ASCD Education Update, 37,* 1-5.

Cox, M. (1990). Interview: Paulo Freire. *Omni, 12,* 75-79, 93-94.

Csikszentmihalyi, M. (1990). *Flow.* New York: HarperPerennial.

Damasio, A. R. (1994). *Descarte's error: Emotion, reason and the human brain.* New York: Grosset/Putnam.

Darling-Hammond, L., & McLaughlin, M. W. (1995). Policies that support professional development in an era of reform. *Phi Delta Kappan, 76,* 597-604.

Davis, S., & Botkin, J. (1994). *The monster under the bed: How business is mastering the opportunity of knowledge for profit.* New York: Simon & Schuster.

Dewey, J. (1915). *The school and society* (Rev. ed.). Chicago: University of Chicago Press.

Dewey, J. (1938). *Experience and education* (12th printing). New York: Collier.

Dilworth, M. E., & Imig, D. G. (1995). Professional teacher development. *The ERIC Review, 3*, 5-11.

EdSource. (1996, February). *EdFact™ fact sheet* (pp. 2-3). Menlo Park, CA: Author.

Ehrlich, P. R., & Ehrlich, A. H. (1996). *Betrayal of science and reason: How anti-environmental rhetoric threatens our future.* Washington, DC: Island.

Ferguson, M. (1980). *The aquarian conspiracy: Personal and social transformation in the 1980s.* Los Angeles: J. P. Tarcher.

Freire, P. (1972). *Pedagogy of the oppressed.* New York: Herder & Herder.

Fullan, M. (1993). *Change forces.* Bristol, PA: Falmer.

Fullan, M., & Hargreaves, A. (Eds.). (1992). *Teacher development and educational change.* Bristol, PA: Falmer.

Fullan, M., with Stiegelbauer, S. (1991). *The new meaning of educational change* (2nd ed.). New York: Teachers College Press.

Furth, H. G. (1970). *Piaget for teachers.* New York: Prentice Hall.

Gardner, H. (1983). *Frames of mind: The theory of multiple intelligences.* New York: Basic Books.

Gardner, H. (1991). *The unschooled mind.* New York: Basic Books.

Gardner, H. (1997, March). *Beyond multiple intelligences.* Paper presented at the the second general session, 52nd Annual Conference of the Association for Supervision and Curriculum Development, Baltimore, MD.

Gates, B. (1995). *The road ahead.* New York: Viking Penguin.

Gatto, J. T. (1992). *Dumbing us down.* Philadelphia, PA: New Society.

Gatto, J. T. (1995). A different kind of teacher. *GATEWAY, 5* (Conf. suppl.), 1-13.

Goodlad, J. I., & Anderson, R. H. (1987). *The non-graded elementary school* (Rev. ed.). New York: Teachers College Press.

Gore, A. (1993). *Earth in the balance: Ecology and the human spirit.* New York: Houghton Mifflin.

Hargreaves, A. (1994). *Changing teachers, changing times: Teachers' work and culture in the postmodern age.* New York: Teachers College Press.

Hart, L. (1983). *Human brain and human learning.* Village of Oak Creek, AZ: Books for Educators.

Healy, J. M. (1990). *Endangered minds: Why our children don't think.* New York: Simon & Schuster.

Herbert, N. (1985). *Quantum reality: Beyond the new physics.* New York: Anchor Press/Doubleday.

Holt, J. (1964). *How children fail.* New York: Pitman.

Kay, A. (1995, October 10). *Powerful ideas need love too!* Unpublished written remarks excerpted from a speech prepared for the Joint

Hearing on Educational Technology in the 21st Century, Science Committee, and the Economic and Educational Opportunities Committee, U.S. House of Representatives.

Kearns, D. T. (1990, Suppl. Spring). Why I got involved. *Fortune*, 46-47.

Kearns, D. T., & Doyle, D. P. (1991). *Winning the brain race: A bold plan to make our schools competitive*. San Francisco: Institute for Contemporary Studies (ICS) Press.

Keyes, K. Jr. (1983). *The hundredth monkey*. Coos Bay, OR: Vision Books.

Kohl, H. R. (1969). *The open classroom: A practical guide to a new way of teaching*. New York: New York Review.

Kovalik, S. (1993). *ITI: The model—Integrated thematic instruction*. Village of Oak Creek, AZ: Books for Educators.

Kovalik, S. (1995). *How to make your classroom brain-compatible* [Cassette Recording No. 95-3210]. Alexandria, VA: Association for Supervision and Curriculum Development.

Kovalik, S., & Olsen, K. (1991). *Kid's-eye view of science: A teacher's handbook for implementing an integrated thematic instruction approach to teaching science, K-6*. Village of Oak Creek, AZ: Center for the Future of Public Education.

Kozol, J. (1990). *The night is dark and I am far from home* (Rev. ed.). New York: Touchstone.

Krashen, S. (1992). *The input hypothesis: Issues and implications*. Torrance, CA: Loredo.

Land, G., & Jarman, B. (1992). *Breakpoint and beyond: Mastering the future—today*. New York: Harper Business.

Lieberman, A. (1995). Practices that support teacher development: Transforming conceptions of professional learning. *Phi Delta Kappan, 76*, 591-596.

Margolin, M. (1989). *Monterey in 1786: The journals of Jean Francois de la Perouse*. Berkeley, CA: Heyday.

McDiarmid, G. W. (1992). Tilting at webs of belief: Field experiences as a means of breaking with experience. In S. Feiman-Nemser & H. Featherstone (Eds.), *Exploring teaching: Reinventing an introductory course* (pp. 34-58). New York: Teachers College Press.

McElvain, C. (1995, Winter). *Study guide for Language Development Specialist certification* (Rev.). (Available from Evergreen School District, 3188 Quimby Road, San Jose, CA 95148).

McLuhan, M. (1964). *Understanding media: The extensions of man*. New York: Signet.

Millman, D. (1980). *The way of the peaceful warrior*. Tiburon, CA: H J Kramer.

Montessori, M. (1956). *The child in the family*. New York: Avon.

Morgan, A. (1983). Theoretical aspects of project-based learning in higher education. *British Journal of Educational Technology, 14,* 66-78.

Muther, C. (1996). *What makes great teachers? How to reveal and nurture greatness* [Cassette Recording No. 96-2117]. Alexandria, VA: Association for Supervision and Curriculum Development.

Naisbitt, J. (1984). *Megatrends: Ten new directions transforming our lives* (Rev. ed.). New York: Warner.

Naisbitt, J. (1994). *Global paradox.* New York: William Morrow.

National Center for Education Statistics. (1994). *Mini-digest of education statistics* (NCES Publication No. 95-163). Washington, DC: U.S. Department of Education, Office of Educational Research and Improvement.

National Center for Education Statistics. (1995). *Projections of education statistics to 2005* (NCES Publication No. 94-131). Washington, DC: U.S. Department of Education, Office of Educational Research and Improvement.

Neill, A. S. (1960). *Summerhill.* New York: Hart.

Office of Educational Research and Improvement (OERI). (1993). *Toward a new science of instruction.* (GPO Publication No. 065-000-00589-1) Washington, DC: U.S. Department of Education.

Pearce, J. C. (1985). *The magical child matures.* New York: E. P. Dutton.

Pinchot, G., & Pinchot, E. (1994). *The end of bureaucracy and the rise of the intelligent organization.* San Francisco: Berrett-Koehler.

Postman, N., & Weingartner, C. (1969). *Teaching as a subversive activity.* New York: Delacorte.

Ray, M., & Rinzler, A. (1993). *The new paradigm in business: Emerging strategies for leadership and organizational change.* New York: J. P. Tarcher.

Robbins, J. (1996). *Reclaiming our health: Exploding the medical myth and embracing the source of true healing.* Tiburon, CA: H J Kramer.

SARK. (1992). *Inspiration sandwich: Stories to inspire our creative freedom.* Berkeley, CA: Celestial Arts.

Schaef, A. W., & Fassel, D. (1990). *The addictive organization: Why we overwork, cover up, pick up the pieces, please the boss & perpetuate sick organizations.* San Francisco: Harper & Row.

Scholtes, P. R. (1988). *The team handbook: How to use teams to improve quality.* Madison, WI: Joiner.

Secretary's Commission on Achieving Necessary Skills (SCANS). (1991). *What work requires of schools* (SSOP ISBN 0-16-035853-1). Washington, DC: U.S. Government Printing Office.

Senge, P. M. (1990). *The fifth discipline: The art and practice of the learning organization.* New York: Doubleday Currency.

Sikes, P. J. (1992). Imposed change and the experienced teacher. In M. Fullan & A. Hargreaves (Eds.), *Teacher development and educational change* (pp. 36-55) Bristol, PA: Falmer.

Smith, F. (1988). *Joining the literacy club.* Portsmouth, NH: Heinemann.

Smith, F. (1995). Let's declare education a disaster and get on with our lives. *Phi Delta Kappan, 76,* 584-590.

Sparks, D. (1995). A paradigm shift in staff development. *The ERIC Review, 3,* 2-4.

Suris, O. (1996, July 18). How Ford cut costs on its 1997 Taurus, little by little. *Wall Street Journal,* pp. B1, B12.

Sylwester, R. (1995). *A celebration of neurons: An educator's guide to the human brain.* Alexandria, VA: Association for Supervision and Curriculum Development.

Toffler, A. (1970). *Future shock.* New York: Random House.

Toffler, A., & Toffler, H. (1995). *Creating a new civilization: The politics of the third wave* (Rev. ed.) Atlanta, GA: Turner.

Walton, M. (1986). *The Deming management method.* New York: Perigee.

Wasley, P. A. (1994). *Stirring the chalkdust.* New York: Teachers College Press.

Wheatley, M. (1992). *Leadership and the new science: Learning about organization from an orderly universe.* San Francisco: Berrett-Koehler.

Wilson, S. M. (1992). Thinking about teaching, teaching about teaching. In S. Feiman-Nemser & H. Featherstone (Eds.), *Exploring teaching: Reinventing an introductory course* (pp. 129-145). New York: Teachers College Press.

Wood, F. H., & Thompson, S. R. (1993). Assumptions about staff development based on research and best practice. *Journal of Staff Development, 14*(4), 52-57.

Zukav, G. (1989). *The seat of the soul.* New York: Simon & Schuster.

Index

CORWIN
PRESS

The Corwin Press logo—a raven striding across an open book—represents the happy union of courage and learning. We are a professional-level publisher of books and journals for K–12 educators, and we are committed to creating and providing resources that embody these qualities. Corwin's motto is "Success for All Learners."